THE STEALING OF AMERICA

The Rutherford Institute

John W. Whitehead is the founder of The Rutherford Institute. The Institute is a non-profit legal and educational organization designed to educate the general public on many of the issues discussed in this book. The Institute is also involved in legal cases that concern free speech and free exercise issues. For further information write:

The Rutherford Institute
P.O. Box 510
Manassas, VA 22110

THE STEALING OF AMERICA

John W. Whitehead

CROSSWAY BOOKS • WESTCHESTER, ILLINOIS
A DIVISION OF GOOD NEWS PUBLISHERS

Cover designed by Ray Cioni/The Cioni Art Works

First printing, 1983

Printed in the United States of America

Library of Congress Catalog Card Number 83-70320

ISBN 0-89107-286-1

To Franky Schaeffer,
A True Friend

ACKNOWLEDGMENTS

Good books are not usually written by committees. There are, however, many people behind every project.

Francis A. Schaeffer's advice and teachings on the essential priorities are reflected in the following pages. Dr. Schaeffer stands as one of the great philosophers of our times.

Franky Schaeffer's creativity, insight, and encouragement were extremely helpful in writing this book. Jim Buchfuehrer's counsel was also of assistance.

Wendell Bird's comments and suggestions on the manuscript were very helpful, as was the editorial work of Jan Dennis. Ray Cioni's design of this book is greatly appreciated.

The typing of the original manuscript was done by my wife, Carol, and also by Pat Dwyer. Carol, along with my children, Jayson, Jonathan, Elisabeth and Joel, were more than patient during the time involved in writing this book.

Finally, I would like to thank the countless people who are courageously struggling to keep freedom intact in America and around the world. Hopefully their efforts will keep the flame of freedom burning.

John W. Whitehead
Manassas, Virginia

CONTENTS

CONTENTS

AUTHOR'S FOREWORD

A deep-felt concern with the serious problems now confronting the American people prompted me to write this book.

All of these problems originate from a single, overriding dilemma: what to do about the dangerous direction of the American government. This is one of *the* most pressing issues of our day.

The assertion of governmental authority over areas of life once considered to be under individual and private control means that the American state has become more than a government. It is making claims and is acting as if it possesses the attributes of deity. It is a state that now claims total ownership. As a result such areas as human life, the family, the church, the school, and private property have become more and more the province of state authorities.

The central issue of governmental power begets other critical questions that a growing number of people are facing for the first time: What nonviolent recourse has a citizenry against a total government that acts oppressively and lawlessly? Moreover, if the citizenry is to act, what are the most strategic and effective steps to take?

Historically Americans have met the challenges before them. The American republic came into existence because the challenges of tyranny were met. However, never before have Americans faced such an onslaught of totalitarian ideas and acts.

The spirit of freedom that made America great, and provided the basis for resistance against tyranny, has been stolen by those who deny that spirit. This is *The Stealing of America*. As a consequence, we now see emerging an aura of fear, oppression, and death. It is the thesis of this book that if the present trends of our government and society are not reversed, then the future hovers between an iron-fisted state and one that conceals the iron fist under a velvet glove.

It is, however, not too late. There is still time. The courses of action to arrest the slide toward the authoritarian state are contained within the pages of this book. If diligently acted upon, there is yet hope for a free future.

Those who do not remember the past are condemned to relive it.

George Santayana

1 A TIME OF PARENTHESIS

We live in a time of parenthesis—with the present age floating in between yesterday and today.

For the first time in its history, the American nation has no idea what its future *ought* to be.

Politically, economically, and morally, America has become a broken reed. The old forms (the glue that bound society together), such as traditional religion and the family, that once predominated, have been shaken.

The idea of absolutes is dead. All things are seen as relative, even the value of human life.

Beset by numerous crises we stand paralyzed, unable to act effectively. As a consequence, our age is characterized by confusion, chaos, and decay.

"You are dying," Oswald Spengler wrote in *The Decline of the West*. "I see in you all the characteristic stigma of decay. I can prove that your great wealth and your great poverty, your capitalism and your socialism, your wars and your revolutions, your atheism and your pessimism and your cynicism, your immorality, your broken-down marriages, your birth control, that is bleeding you from the bottom and killing you off at the top in your brains—can prove to you that these are characteristic marks of the dying ages of ancient states—Alexandria and Greece and neurotic Rome."[1]

Some, on the other hand, such as Alvin Toffler in his book *The Third Wave* believe that the human race stands on the dawn of a new civilization.[2] Indeed, man now has the ability to transform not only society but also man himself. At the very same time, he possesses the awesome power to annihilate himself.

1

Modern science with its genetic engineering, "test-tube babies," amniocentesis, sociobiology, and behaviorism has reopened Pandora's box. Science is outrunning the human spirit; man is becoming obsolete. A "brave new world" hovers in the wings of man and of our civilization. But it is no new golden age. It is merely the old tyranny resuscitated by an inhumane science.

Man is fast becoming irrelevant. Compared to the computer, what is man's worth? Is a man qualitatively different than a thinking machine? After all, *Time* magazine nominated the computer as its 1982 "man" of the year.

These are questions that our society cannot answer for the simple reason that man, as man, has been defined away. (He has become but a shadow of his former self, a reflection of his environment.) That is to say, *our modern culture has no view of man in the traditional sense.*

Once thought to be fearfully and wonderfully made in the image of God, man is now a spare part in an inhuman technological machine. He has become unnecessary, a despoiler in an otherwise pristine "nature."

This reduced view of man is clearly reflected in the callous indifference that has developed toward human life. Nowhere is man's disposability more dramatically illustrated than in the case of *Infant Doe.* In that case the Indiana Supreme Court upheld a lower court's decision giving the parents of a newborn infant, who had some congenital defects, the authority to allow the baby to die. After withholding food for six days, the child did indeed starve to death. Clearly, the distinctions between life and nonlife have been blurred.

The older Christian idea that man has dignity and worth is gone. That is precisely the argument of Harvard behaviorist B. F. Skinner in his book, *Beyond Freedom and Dignity.*[3] Skinner once argued that there was hope for man through a controlled environment monitored by a manipulative statist elite. Now, however, in his new pessimism, Skinner sees no hope at all for the human race.[4] To him, mankind is unredeemable.

Media analyst Marshall McLuhan once said that American society moved into 1984 in the 1930s, except no one noticed. The basic groundwork (ideas and technology) for the modern authoritarian state had been laid by the early thirties. All that was needed was someone or something to put the necessary elements together for control of the people. The trend toward worldwide authoritarian regimes had begun. However, the modern regimes differ in kind from the older ones because government has become much more pervasive; it controls more of the totality of life.

Today in America many signs indicate that the breakdown of hierarchy—a precondition of totalitarianism—is already underway. America is obviously in a period of disorientation—a time of parenthesis. The basic building blocks of society are being dismantled. As Malcolm Muggeridge writes in *The End of Christendom:* "The whole social structure is now tumbling down, dethroning its God, undermining all its certainties. All this, wonderfully enough, is being done in the name of the health, wealth, and happiness of all mankind."[5]

The Stamping Boot

"If you want a picture of the future," George Orwell wrote some thirty years ago, "imagine a boot stamping on a human face—forever."[6]

In a time when terrorists play death games with hostages, as embassies burn and storm troopers lace up their boots in many lands, it seems that Orwell's vision of the future is being played out in our time.

Increasingly in the twentieth century men have been seeking order in the state. Although some states profess an intention to serve the people, seldom has this been the result of government. To the contrary, power has tended to corrupt those who grasp its reins.

During the past half century, the world has witnessed the rapid rise of totalitarian states with their controlled, monolithic societies. Even in the "free" West we have seen diversity exchanged for an apathetic monolithic sameness.

The growth and power of the state is the most significant political development of the twentieth century.[7] By 1950, what has commonly been called the "free world" had shrunk from over 90 to less than 70 percent of the world's population. By 1980, the number of Communist regimes had reached twenty-five, almost twice the total that existed in 1950. Before the year 2000—if current trends continue—the ratio between freedom and communism may well shrink from 65:35 to 50:50. The implications of such a shift are enormous.[8]

The world is moving inexorably toward statism—that is, government seen as a total, final solution to man's problems. Even our own governmental systems are being affected. Ideas do have consequences, and some of those consequences are just now emerging.

What we see in the Soviet Union today is the prototype for the general development of the state in our modern world, with its attendant growth and structure. To be sure, we are aware of all the differences that may exist between the Soviet state and the American state, or for instance, the British or French states— such as constitutional and other practical differences. However, as Jacques Ellul notes:

> They exist, but are of little consequence compared with the similarities, and particularly with the general trend. *There are more differences between the American state of 1910 and that of 1960 (despite the constitutional sameness) than between the latter and the Soviet state (despite the constitutional differences).*[9]

As the stamping boot of totalitarianism casts its ominous shadow around us, we must be concerned, not only with foreign enemies, but also with the signs of authoritarianism and monolithic sameness revealing themselves today in America. As former presidential advisor Bertram Gross has remarked: "As I look at America today, I am not afraid to say that I am afraid."[10]

People intuitively sense that we of the present era are in danger of being consumed by the authoritarian state. A few years ago political scientist Kenneth Dolbeare conducted a series of indepth interviews totaling twenty-five hours per person. He found that most respondents were deeply afraid of some future statist authoritarianism. "The most striking thing about inquiring into expectations for the future," he reported, "is the rapidity with which the concept of fascism (with or without the label) enters the conversation."[11]

However, anyone looking for black shirts, mass rallies, or men on horseback will miss the telltale clues of what Gross calls "creeping fascism."[12]

In America, it [will] be supermodern and multiethnic—as American as Madison Avenue, executive luncheons, credit cards, and apple pie. It [will] be fascism with a smile. As a warning against its cosmetic facade, subtle manipulation, and velvet gloves, I call it friendly fascism. What scares me most is its subtle appeal.[13]

The typical response is that fascism is not possible in the current leftward drift of society. But that leftward drift is precisely what makes fascism an imminent threat, because fascism is and always has been a leftist ideology. It is simply *nationalistic socialism*, in contrast to *international socialism*, which is Marxism.

Thus, the crude old forms of totalitarianism will most likely not come to fruition in America, but something more deadly and subtle. As Francis Schaeffer writes: "We must think rather of a *manipulative* authoritarian government. Modern governments have forms of manipulation at their disposal which the world has never known before."[14] For example, Hitler was awesome, but think what he could have accomplished if television had been available to him—or, for that matter, if other modern technological devices, such as the computer, had been at his disposal. Although television and computers are not inherently dangerous, they can be potent weapons of manipulation and control in the hands of a power-hungry ruler.

Political analyst Kevin Phillips would agree that if authoritarianism develops further in this country, it will not be of the obvious Hitler brand.[15] However, this should not lead us to believe that the results of a manipulative authoritarian government would be finally different from the type that Hitler established. *In the end, all authoritarian regimes, even the "benevolent" type, arrive at the same antihuman point.*

Therefore, in the United States we must not think of an overnight change, but rather of a subtle trend by those in leadership—government, media, education—toward greater control and manipulation of the individual. With the advent of the electronic media, the mechanism for manipulation has arrived. The electronic media, Franky Schaeffer argues, is the "one group more than any other" that "forms public opinions."[16] The media more than forms public opinion, however; *it alters the consciousness and world view of entire populations.*

Sweden, for example, has shown us that relatively crude indoctrination by television and public education holds tremendous possibilities for the authoritarian state. The Swedes through the medium of television have also demonstrated a kind of powerful semantic manipulation, not unlike Orwell's Newspeak, in which words are more or less gradually changed to mean something else. In this way undesirable concepts can be done away with.

As journalist Roland Huntford demonstrates in *The New Totalitarians,* the word *freedom* does not yet in Swedish mean exactly "slavery." It does, however, already imply "submission," thereby being effectively neutralized as a rallying word in the vocabulary of forces that oppose servitude to the state.[17]

The world, it must be remembered, has not been terrorized by despots advertising themselves as devils. Instead, the totalitarian regimes have come to power while reciting platitudes of liberty, equality, and fraternity. This was true of the French Revolution and the Russian Revolution, and is equally true of modern communism and third-world socialism.

Some might feel uncomfortable about increased government control and manipulation, but as our modern secular culture descends upon them, where will they draw the line? Moreover, many who speak of civil liberties are also committed to the concept of the state's authority and responsibility to solve all problems. Therefore, in a time of overwhelming pressures, at some point the feeling of discomfort will be submerged.

There is still enough of the older ethical base—what has been called the Christian memory—that the American people will rebel if they consciously realize what is happening. But if this trend toward control continues to move slowly, there will most likely be little resistance.

As the state gradually assumes more control, calls to the people for allegiance will come from the right and the left. However, when and if the authoritarian curtain falls, as Francis Schaeffer notes, "the words *left* or *right* will make no difference. In their extreme forms they are only two roads to the same end. There is no difference between an authoritarian government from the right or the left: the results are the same."[18]

Modern men and women are beginning to feel the strain of

the unmanageability of their lives. With this hopelessness they seem to be surrendering their minds and their civil liberties to those who "can explain the world anew."[19] As William Irwin Thompson puts it, "When the individual's consciousness is made up of a moving collage of televised fragments, his state of anxiety makes him prey to 'the recollectivization through terror' of the fascist state."[20] Therefore, helpless before the monster of technology he has created, man in an act of faith surrenders to the power of explanation given him by way of its mouthpiece, the media.

Off in the distance, we can hear the stamping boot coming closer and closer. It is the same old boot but with a velvet touch. And this time it is stamping to the beat of a different drummer.

"There is no reason," Aldous Huxley once wrote, "why the new totalitarian should resemble the old. Government by firing squads . . . is not merely inhumane . . . it is demonstrably inefficient, and in an age of advanced technology, inefficiency is a sin against the Holy Ghost. A really efficient totalitarian state would be one in which the all-powerful executive of political bosses and their army of managers control a population of slaves who do not have to be coerced because they love their servitude."[21]

Those in servitude are slaves, and slaves are the property of their masters. *They are owned.* As modern men look to the state as the source of rights and bread, increasingly they too become slaves to the governmental elite.

As all false gods, however, the state requires sacrifice to be made to it. The sacrifice it requires is indeed a most precious item—freedom.

2 ON THE ROAD TO AUSCHWITZ

The signs at the entrances merely said "BATHS." They were not sinister looking places at all, especially with the well-kept lawns and flower borders.

The music was sweet and light—even beautiful. One survivor recalled that an orchestra of "young and pretty girls all dressed in white blouses and navy-blue skirts" played the music.

The place? The gas chambers at the Nazi concentration camp at Auschwitz. William Shirer in *The Rise and Fall of the Third Reich* describes what happened to the unsuspecting Jews who thought they were simply being taken to the baths for delousing (which was customary at all concentration camps).

To music, "recalling as it did happier and more frivolous times, the men, women and children were led into the 'bath houses,' where they were told to undress preparatory to taking a 'shower.' Sometimes they were given towels. Once they were inside the 'shower-room'—and perhaps this was the first moment that they may have suspected something was amiss, for as many as two thousand of them were packed into the chamber like sardines, making it difficult to take a bath—the massive door was slid shut, locked and hermetically sealed. Up above where the well-groomed lawn and flower beds almost concealed the mushroom-shaped lids of vents that ran up from the hall of death, orderlies stood ready to drop into them the amethyst-blue crystals of hydrogen cyanide. . . .

"Surviving prisoners watching from blocks nearby remembered how for a time the signal for the orderlies to pour the crystals down the vents was given by a Sergeant Moll. *'Na, gib ihnen schon zu fressen'* ('Alright, give 'em something to chew on'), he would laugh and the crystals would be poured through the openings, which were then sealed.

"Through heavy-glass portholes the executioners could watch what happened. The naked prisoners below would be looking up at the showers from which no water spouted or perhaps at the floor wondering why there were no drains. It took some moments for the gas to have much effect. But soon the inmates became aware that it was issuing from the perforations in the vents. It was then that they usually panicked, crowding away from the pipes and finally stampeding toward the huge metal door where . . . 'they piled up in one blue clammy blood-spattered pyramid, clawing and mauling each other even in death.' "[1]

Luther's Ideas

Before we can even begin analyzing the cause of the death camps, one key fact must be realized. The German people who, at least by silent acquiescence, condoned the horrors of Auschwitz were not a tribe of savages.

In fact, the acts described above "were the official, legal acts and policies of modern Germany—an educated, industrialized, *civilized* Western European nation, a nation renowned throughout the world for the luster of its intellectual and cultural achievements."[2] It was a country the Germans proudly called "the land of poets and philosophers." But it was a country that would offer no protection against the likes of Sergeant Moll.

Ideas. That is what brought Germany to the death camps— ideas that proved to be destructive.

Governments, regimes, societal shifts, and such are always preceded by ideas and philosophy. The consequences of ideas cannot be overemphasized.

With the predominance of the electronic media, "ideas and symbols," Michael Novak writes, "have become more powerful than reality. They are the *new* reality."[3] Moreover, a philosophy or world view, as it is placed into the cultural thought forms and gains prominence, paves the way for what follows. Ideas, thus, have the capacity for producing good or evil consequences.

Ideas developed by Martin Luther gave the world a sense of freedom. Hailing from Germany, Luther in the early 1500s led the way for the Reformation. Luther rediscovered and reinterpreted certain doctrines and ideas already held by the Roman Catholic Church. He probably pushed these ideas further than the Roman Catholic Church would have. Luther's recycled ideas prevailed in Germany in Western Europe up to the early nineteenth century.

Two important views emerged from Luther's theology and philosophy that altered the concept of truth virtually unknown in his time.

First, Luther argued that *the Bible was the final authority*. Nothing was considered superior or even equal to it in authority. This meant that man and all his institutions, including the state as well as the church, were *under* the authority of God and the Bible.

As such, all of life was subject to a system of moral absolutes. This doctrine gave to the world a new sense of *responsibility;* that is, man and his institutions are responsible to the Creator for their acts. This doctrine also imposed *limitations on the state;* that is, government received its authority from God and was subject to God. Citizens also received rights from God and were not mere vassals of the state.

Second, perhaps more profound for most sixteenth-century institutions, was Luther's argument for *the priesthood of all believers*. Up to this point in time, men passed through hierarchies and mediators as the pathway to God. Luther's doctrine attacked this idea. He asserted that all men, without need of a king (claiming divine rights) or any other human agency, had immediate access to God. This doctrine gave us *individualism* (but with responsibility).

Individual responsibility was a basic building block of the free nations that followed the Reformation. It broke down hierarchies and gave man not only immediate access to God but also equality with all other men before God. This meant that even the man on the street could call the king to task as based upon the absolutes of the Bible.

The importance of these principles lies in this basic axiom: If individual responsibility is denied, hierarchies fill the vacuum that remains. The tragedy of the pre-Nazi German church and Christians was their failure to maintain the predominance of these concepts in their society—much the same way the American church has failed to maintain these principles today.

Kant and Hegel

The shift in the ideas of truth in Germany was brought about by several key philosophers who came along after Luther. Immanuel Kant (1724-1804) and Georg Wilhelm Friedrich Hegel (1770-1831), both German, brought the new philosophies and thought forms into the German culture. These thought forms, imported into our country in the early twentieth century, now hold a place of prominence in some of the major institutions of American society.

Kant is the father of the Romanticist movement. He claimed to have proved for the first time that existence is in principle unknowable to man's mind.

Those who followed Kant held, in principle, that man's mind (and the use of reason) is unable to acquire any knowledge of reality. The real world, according to Kantian philosophy, is subjective; that is, the world is merely what man perceives it to be.

Kant's idea has such profound impact because it means that there is no objective existence of the Creator or of truth. In his view then, this would mean that the Creator and truth are essentially unknowable.

Hegel's philosophy was the next crucial step beyond Kant. Men up to the time of Hegel thought in terms of *antithesis;* that is, A cannot be non-A, evil cannot be good. Therefore, prior to Hegel men thought in terms of absolutes, on the assumption that there were such things as absolute good and evil. There was a tension or conflict between truth and nontruth.

Hegel changed the rules of the game by offering a solution to the conflict. The answer, he said, would be quite simple if people would stop thinking in terms of antithesis. Instead, think in terms of synthesis, something different from both thesis and antithesis. The apparent absolutes would both be wrong. Moreover, the new synthesis would not be an absolute, because an antithesis to it would arise, from which a new synthesis would develop. This was a perpetual and ongoing process with one thesis and one antithesis after another producing synthesis after synthesis.

Hegel believed the tension would always be present with the two realms (thesis-antithesis) contradicting each other. As a consequence of the *contradiction* and its conflicting *opposites,* a *synthesis* would result. An example of Hegel's triad solution to the tension is diagrammed as follows:

Yes   1. Contradiction   No
                    2. Conflict
                    3. Synthesis

                     Maybe

An idea or situation always potentially contains its opposite, develops it, struggles against it, and then unites with it to take another form or synthesis.

Hegel applied synthesis to being, or existence. The opposite of *being* is *nonbeing*. Contradiction here develops a conflict between the two concepts which produces synthesis. The result of synthesis is *becoming*.

This places everything into perpetual motion. Nothing is ever being or existing, but is always becoming. Man, as a person, does not exist, but is only becoming. Under such a system of thought, facts and even life are expressed in *potentiality.* This philosophy made it easy for the United States Supreme Court to label unborn children "potential life" in the 1973 case of *Roe v. Wade.*

Hegel's dialectic logic obliterates the ideas of an objective God, of absolute truth, and of moral absolutes. Everything is relative. The situation which produces the synthesis is the critical point; there is no objective truth behind the situation. God is dead; truth is lost; morals are relative.

Distinctions of any kind, Hegel held, are unreal. A is non-A, being is also nonbeing. Thus, everything is one, and the things of this world—which subjectively appear to be individual—are merely partial aspects of one all-consuming whole which Hegel called the Absolute. The "Absolute" was best represented here on earth by the state (or government) to which all "individuals" are subordinate.[4]

"[A]ll worth which the human being possesses," Hegel wrote, "all spiritual reality, he possesses only through the State."[5] The state, then, becomes, in effect, God walking on earth and has the "supreme right against the individual, whose supreme duty is to be a member of the state."[6]

Three Ideas

Essentially the philosophy of Kant and Hegel can be summarized in two terms: *pragmatism* and *collectivism*. Hitler added a third solidifying idea to this matrix: social and political *evolution*. Pragmatism is the idea that if something has utility (if it works) then it should be put into effect. In *Mein Kampf* Hitler writes that "everything must be examined from this point of view and used or rejected according to its utility."[7] Or as one of Hitler's major spokesmen, Joseph Goebbels, put it: "Important is not what is right but what wins."[8]

Pragmatism means that there is no such thing as absolute truth. Pragmatism thus leads to *relativism*, which holds that an idea or action must be judged as true or false according to its utility in a particular situation. Relativism is based on the assumption, propounded by Kant and Hegel, that there is no truth and there are no absolutes. This philosophy is reflected in such contemporary concepts as situational ethics and values clarification. What works today in one situation may not work tomorrow in another situation. Everything is arbitrary depending on its usefulness.

Collectivism is the idea that the group (the collective) has primacy over the individual. In other words, the wishes of the majority are more important than the wishes of an individual, even if the effect is deprivation of that individual's freedom. Under collectivism the collective—society, the community, the nation, the proletariat, etc.—is *"the unit of reality and the standard of value."*[9] This means that the individual has reality only as part of the group, and value only insofar as he serves it. The individual "is to be sacrificed for the group whenever it—or its representative, the state—deems this desirable."[10] The state then becomes all-powerful; politically this is a dictatorship, and economically it is socialism.

In following Hegel, the Nazis asserted that the people have to "realize that the State is more important than the individual, that individuals must be willing and ready to sacrifice themselves for Nation and Führer."[11] Mankind is seen as a mass (or the masses), and the human leaders become the gods, the führers.

Luther's idea that the Creator stands over the state and that the individual has access to the Creator is directly contradictory to and is undermined by pragmatism and collectivism. Without the same ideas as Luther's, the framers of the Declaration of Independence could not have appealed to the Creator in restricting the tyranny of Great Britain. Deprived of Luther's philosophy (because of the encroachment of liberal theology), the German people were, in effect, helpless to stop the authoritarian state that Hitler represented.

Collectivism, it must be understood, reduces man's individual responsibility and shifts it to the group. As in Germany, responsibility is then not seen as a duty owed to the Creator but to the state.

The third idea, evolution, is one of the most influential in the history of mankind. It has totally transformed the thoughts and actions of the men and women who have followed its ramifications in science, theology, social studies, and government.

Indeed, Social Darwinism (that is, evolution applied to society) provided in part an indispensable basis for fascism and its oppressive racist actions. Evolution pervaded Mussolini's thinking to the point that he justified war on the basis that it provided the means for evolutionary progress.[12]

Charles Darwin himself provided the racist element of the theory of evolution. His earthshaking book is often cited as *The Origin of the Species*. However, the complete title of the work is *The Origin of the Species by Means of Natural Selection or the Preservation of Favoured Races in the Struggle for Life*—the favored race being, of course, the white race.[13] In fact Harvard biologist Stephen Jay Gould, an evolutionist himself, has recently documented the racism that has historically pervaded evolutionary thinking.[14]

One need not read far in Hitler's *Mein Kampf* to find that evolution likewise influenced him and his views on the master race, genocide, and human breeding experiments. Arthur Keith, an evolutionary anthropologist, said of Hitler: "The German Führer . . . has consciously sought to make the practice of Germany conform to the theory of evolution."[15]

Paving the Way

In Germany the ideas of Kant and Hegel culminated in Hitler and also Stalin, who both fitted these ideas into their deterministic belief in evolution. "The needs of the state," Hitler proclaimed, "are the sole determining factor. What may be necessary today need not be so tomorrow. This is not a question of theoretical suppositions, but of practical decisions dictated by existing circumstances. Therefore, I may—nay, must—change or repudiate under changed conditions tomorrow what I consider correct today."[16] This is relativism.

Why this power? Because Hitler represented the Absolute. As a spokesman of the Nazi party declared in 1933: "The authority of the Führer is not limited by checks and controls, by special autonomous bodies or individual rights, but it is free and independent, all-inclusive and unlimited."[17]

On October 7, 1933 Hitler said, "It is thus necessary that the individual should finally come to realize that his own ego is of no importance in comparison with the existence of his nation, that the position of the individual ego is conditioned solely by the interests of the nation as a whole."[18] This is collectivism, or socialism as we now term it politically.

Under this philosophy all life became relative. If, as it did, it became convenient to exterminate people at Auschwitz, it was done. This was still easier to do with evolution as a foundation. After all, man is yet an evolving animal.

The Jews, labeled subhumans, became nonbeings. It was both legal and right to exterminate them in the collectivist and evolutionist viewpoint. They were not considered part of the whole and thus were not persons in the sight of the German government.

The shift in truth was so complete that the German people actually welcomed Hitler. We must not forget that the Nazi party was elected to office, under a constitutional government, by the freely cast ballots of millions of German voters, including people on every social, economic, and educational level.

On January 30, 1933, in full accordance with the country's legal and constitutional principles, Hitler was appointed chancellor. When German President Hindenburg died in August 1934, Hitler assumed the office of president as well as that of chancellor, but he preferred to use the title *Der Füehrer* (the leader) to describe himself. This new move was approved in a general election in which Hitler obtained 88 percent of the votes cast.[19]

The German people were clearly not ignorant of Hitler's goals when they voted for him. The voters were very aware of the Nazi ideology. Nazi literature, including statements of the Nazi plans for the future, had papered the country for a decade before Hitler came to power. In fact, Hitler's book *Mein Kampf* (1925), which is his blueprint for totalitarianism, sold more than 200,000 copies between 1925 and 1932.

The essence of the political system which Hitler intended to establish in Germany was clear. Thus, the German people, in essence, asked for Auschwitz.

The American Collective

Our country, as it has moved toward a post-Christian consensus, has adopted pragmatic relativism and collectivism as basic themes of American society. Evolution pervades all fields of knowledge. Sir Julian Huxley has written:

> The whole of evolution was soon extended into other than biological fields. Inorganic subjects such as the life-histories of stars and the formation of chemical elements on the one hand, and on the other hand subjects like linguistics, social anthropology, and comparative law and religion, began to be studied from an evolutionary angle, until today we are enabled to see evolution as a universal, all-pervading process.[20]

A consequence of these ideas has been the shift from individual responsibility to a societal responsibility for all acts in American society. This is widely seen as a good thing. For example, prevalent today is the idea that criminals are not responsible for their behavior. Society is to blame. As a result criminal rights are minutely protected while a victim's rights are often ignored.

There is also no-fault divorce and no-fault insurance. This philosophy is devastating because it shifts guilt to society (the collective) from the individual. Killing or other crimes become much easier to commit if there is no guilt and responsibility.

Much of this thinking originated from the pragmatic collectivism that has, over the past fifty years, been taught in the state-financed public educational system. John Dewey, titled the "father of American progressive education," is largely responsible for the philosophy that dominates public education today. Although many educators have had a profound impact on public education, Dewey is unquestionably the most important of the twentieth-century educators.

Dewey was an early convert to Darwinism. He set out to make systematic application of evolutionary concepts to the curriculum and methodology of public education.

In essence, Dewey believed that the evolutionary process had finally reached a state of development in which man could control his own evolution. This could be best initiated through the educational system. For example, he once wrote that "the school as a social center means the active and organized promotion of this socialism of the intangible things of art, science, and other modes of social intercourse."[21] The school as a social center, Dewey believed, would produce a better "social animal."

Dewey was also an early convert to the German philosophers, most principally Hegel. In fact, Dewey was a "disciple" of Hegel "in the early years of his life."[22]

Accordingly, Dewey taught that there is no such thing as a truly distinctive individual. A man's intelligence, he urged, "is fundamentally conditioned by the collective thinking of other men; the mind is not a 'private' phenomenon, it is a social phenomenon."[23] Man's mind becomes public property, an element of the collective.

The true reality, then, is not the individual but society. Truth becomes that which works for the group. Both Kant and Hegel are clearly recognizable in Dewey's thought, as they were in Hitler's.

Dewey's collectivist orientation naturally led to his being a Socialist and an apologist for communism. If Americans were to "reconstruct" society properly, wrote Dewey at the start of the Depression, it "would signify that we had entered constructively and voluntarily upon the road which Soviet Russia is traveling with so much attendant destruction and coercion."[24]

Dewey, however, was not a Marxist. He described himself as a liberal democrat. Although he disagreed with the Bolsheviks on the method of travel, he did not disagree on the final road or ultimate direction.

As a religious humanist Dewey had difficulty in distinguishing religion and education.[25] It was his belief that the public schools could best serve the cause of religion through social unification. He wrote:

> [U]nder certain conditions schools are more religious in substance and in promise without any of the conventional badges and machinery of religious instruction than they could be in cultivating these forms at the expense of a state-consciousness.[26]

The consequence of Dewey's philosophy is obvious: the state schools are to produce people who seek to serve the collective in the betterment of humanity. This means that the individual, in the perpetuation of the "state-consciousness," must submit himself to the collective—that is, the state.

Newton Edwards, a professor of education at the University of Chicago, has summarized the theory underpinning modern public education. He writes:

> Public education is not merely a function of government; it is of government. Power to maintain a system of public schools is an attitude of government in much the same sense as is the police power or the power to administer or to maintain military forces or to tax. . . . The primary function of the public school, in legal theory at least, is not to confer benefits upon the individual as such, the school exists as a state institution because the very existence of civil society demands it.[27]

Thus, in Edwards's view (and that generally accepted by proponents of public education and backed by numerous court decisions) it is the state that has the "right" to educate the youth. Why? This, as Edwards emphasizes, ensures the survival of the state.

Survival of the state, however, necessitates a public school system which, in part, will have to *indoctrinate* its students in what the state believes to be important. "[O]ne of public education's principal functions," writes one legal scholar, "always has been to indoctrinate a generation of children with the values, traditions, and virtues of society."[28] This process is called socialization and it "occurs not only in the family, but also in the public education system."[29]

With few exceptions, today's leading educational and legal scholars have concurred with Professor Edwards. The courts, too, have uniformly affirmed this philosophy. Thus, it has become a part of American law.

For example, the Supreme Court of Kentucky as early as 1909 likened the education of the state's youth to the preparation of the nation's youth for war:

> [Public education] is regarded as an essential to the preservation of liberty—as forming one of the first duties of a democratic government. . . . If it is essentially a prerogative of sovereignty to raise troops in time of war, it is equally so to prepare each generation of youth to discharge the duties of citizenship in time of peace and war. . . . [T]he power to educate the youth of the state [is] so that the state may prosper. . . . It may be doubted if the state could strip itself of either quality of its sovereignty.[30]

In a 1948 case outlawing certain religious exercises in the public schools, Supreme Court Justice Felix Frankfurter stated that the public schools had opted for "secular education" in "recognition of the need of a democratic society to educate its children . . . in an atmosphere free from pressures . . . to serve as perhaps the most powerful agency for promoting cohesion among a heterogeneous democratic people."[31]

The "cohesion" Frankfurter speaks of is the collective, and public education has been the tool in promoting the collective. Public education is, as the Supreme Court affirmed in 1954, "the most important function of the state."[32]

The awesome authority of the public education system cannot be underestimated in its impact on modern society. What people think and do in the real world *is* a product of their education.

In light of the pragmatic collectivism that undergirds modern public education, it is instructive to consider the mentality of some of today's university students. Dr. Richard M. Hunt, associate dean of Harvard University's Graduate School of Arts and Science, tells us of his experience:

> I have taught courses at Harvard for many years. I used to teach these courses from a straight historical perspective. Recently, I tried a new approach and I call the course, "Moral Dilemma in a Repressive Society: Nazi Germany." Through case studies of issues and personalities I try to present the Nazi phenomenon from

the inside, so to speak, from the experience and testimony of those who lived through the period as victims, victimizers, bystanders, true believers, and members of the resistance.

To make a long story short, I was greatly surprised with the reaction of the students. I had asked for personal interpretations of moral relevant dilemmas. In their end-of-term papers, it was not a matter of indifference to Nazi oppressions that I found. Nobody attempted to minimize or explain away Nazi excesses.

Rather what struck me most forcibly were the depressing fatalistic conclusions about major moral dilemmas facing the German people of that particular place and time in history.

Comments like these were frequent. "And with the ever present threat of Gestapo terror, who would dare to speak out and resist? Would you? Would I? Probably not!"

Most disturbing of all to me was the end of the line of such arguments. This point was reached by a few students who seemed somehow to realize the moral peril of such exculpatory judgments. Their way out was to lessen the responsibility of any individual person by dispersing the guilt among all.

Clearly some trends of our times seemed to be running towards a no-fault, that is, a guilt-free society. One might say the virtues of responsible choice, paying the penalty, taking the consequences, all appear at low ebb today.

Next time I teach this course, I hope to stress more strongly my own belief in the contingencies, the open-endedness of history. Somehow, I have got to convey the meaning of moral decisions and their relation to significant outcomes. Most important, I want to point out that single acts of individuals and strong stands of institutions at an early date do make a difference in the long run. I am through with teaching no-fault history.[33]

All Patients Are We

If man is deprived of his individuality and the responsibility for his acts, then he becomes something less than man. He is something to be owned like a slave, or, in modern terms, a patient. As C. S. Lewis observed:

> [T]he concept of dessert [deserving] is the only connecting link between punishment and justice. . . . Thus when we cease to consider what the criminal deserves and consider only what will cure him . . . we have tacitly removed him from the sphere of justice altogether; instead of a person, a subject of rights, we now have a mere object, a patient, "a case."[34]

Without individuality and responsibility, we fade into the collective mass man to become patients, consumers, and numbers in some nondescript computer program. Even criminality is given a new definition. It becomes the group or person that violates the "common interest of society."

In ancient Rome Christians were fed to the lions as criminals for violating the common interest of Roman society. In this century, the Jews have often been singled out for "disrupting" society and have been made scapegoats. In recent years, we have witnessed the extermination of both born and unborn children because their births could violate the imagined common interest of society in "the right of women to control their own bodies." In the end, it means that all of us are at the disposal of the likes of abortionists or a Sergeant Moll and that we are on the road to Auschwitz.

3 SOME OMINOUS PARALLELS

Leonard Peikoff, a former philosophy professor at New York University, in *The Ominous Parallels* suggests that the conditions that existed in pre-Nazi Germany, in an obviously enlightened and cultured German society, are strikingly similar to the present cultural atmosphere in the United States.

Others such as political analyst Kevin Phillips in *Post-Conservative America* see the parallels but caution that they have not yet completely developed.[1] However, the fact that parallels do exist should be enough to cause concern.

Phillips discusses four basic parallels, and I would add a fifth:

1. Economic destabilization
2. Public loss of faith in political and governmental institutions
3. Loss of a war, which strikes at the heart of a nation's and a culture's self-esteem and faith in old verities
4. Loss of traditional value structures
5. The devaluation of human life.

Economic Destabilization

If the economy does not respond in the 1980s, then political and economic upheaval seem certain.

Inflation is a major cause of economic destabilization. Massive inflation in pre-Nazi Germany is most often blamed for the rise of Hitler. The reason is that it destroyed prosperity and affluence, which made people desperate for *any* solution and willing to sacrifice principle. As the 1923 German inflation peaked, suitcases of currency, *billionen* of marks, were needed to buy groceries.

22

Massive inflation has preceded too many of the other totalitarian regimes of this century to be dismissed as unimportant. For example, in 1946 the Hungarian government's central bank printed the 10-quintrillion Pengo note which, before the Second World War, would have bought the whole country. In April 1946 a 10-quintrillion Pengo note could not purchase a dozen eggs. With the collapse of the Hungarian economy, of course, came Communist dictatorship.

In 1949 China was drowned in an inflation almost identical to that in pre-Nazi Germany. It resulted in Mao Tse-tung's authoritarian dictatorship. And so on, globally.

The first wave of peacetime double-digit inflation hit the United States from 1973 to 1975. The second wave, occurring from 1979 to 1980, was even worse.

Of course such inflation does not match what occurred in pre-Nazi Germany. "However, the inflation we have had has been insidious, wearing down morality, productivity and support for existing institutions—as it always does."[2] As Phillips notes, "No one can safely assume that inflation must reach the levels of [Germany] to lay the groundwork for political upheaval."[3]

Alvin Toffler in *The Third Wave* sees the present economic crisis in terms of three waves of thought and invention. The first wave was unleashed 10,000 years ago, he says, by the invention of agriculture. The second wave of change touched off the industrial revolution and gave us the factory.

The third wave is the information age, epitomized by the computer revolution. Toffler writes: "Tearing our families apart, rocking our economy, paralyzing our political systems, shattering our values, the Third Wave affects everyone."[4]

Critical to understanding the crisis in American culture today is the shift that has occurred from an industrial to an informational society. That is, a move from a second- to a third-wave society has occurred, or what Harvard sociologist Daniel Bell has termed the postindustrial society.

With the emergence of computers and microprocessors, we have entered a new course of change. However, as social analyst John Naisbitt writes: "Change is occurring so rapidly that there is no time to react."[5]

The reality of what is happening is perhaps best illustrated by the automobile industry. It is a second-wave industry that is being slowly phased out by the predominance of the information business. As Naisbitt notes: "Many automobile companies are just not going to survive. . . . The thirty automobile companies now competing . . . will, by the end of the 1980s, be reduced to as few as seven to eight companies or alliances of companies."[6]

Anyone who knows American business knows that the automobile industry is one of several industries that form the backbone of our economy. That backbone is disintegrating.

Thus, the economic upheaval could worsen. Unfortunately, as Francis Schaeffer observes, people vote their pocketbooks to protect their personal peace and affluence. The economic factor is definitely a very real parallel.

Public Loss of Faith in Political and Governmental Institutions

A second major parallel is a public loss of faith in political and governmental institutions. In pre-Nazi Germany, under the Weimar Constitution the people had, in a drastic fashion, lost any trust in their governmental structure.

Likewise, there has been a collapse of the American public's faith in its major institutions such as the presidency, the Congress, the Supreme Court, the executive branch, and political parties. One might do well to consider the cumulative historical impact of events from the assassination of John F. Kennedy in 1963 to the forced resignation of Richard Nixon in 1974. They have left fragmentation, violence, and rejection of values.

Several observers—such as columnist Stewart Alsop and historian Hugh Trevor-Roper—have likened the toppling of Richard Nixon to the overthrows of England's King Charles I and France's Louis XVI.[7] If one accepts Nixon's overthrow as a republican form of regicide, then apt historical analogies come into play.

All Western powers have seen the popular overthrow or execution of kings at some crucial point in their history. As Phillips notes:

> In each case, there followed a relatively short period, from a year or so to a decade, of attempted democratic rule through a legisla-

ture . . . the final phase invariably produced an authoritarian regime and the great symbolic strongmen of modern history: Oliver Cromwell, Napoleon Bonaparte, Nikolai Lenin, Adolf Hitler, Francisco Franco. Arguably, the United States has already pursued a very limited version of such progression.[8]

Americans have also lost respect for their legal and political systems. However, one *cannot* understand the demise of law and politics today without recognizing the demise of the Constitution; *in America we no longer operate under a written Constitution.* Rule of law, the bedrock of the Constitution, has been replaced by rule of men.

"[T]he Constitution," Supreme Court Chief Justice Charles Evans Hughes once remarked, "is what the judges say it is."[9] As I have noted elsewhere, by way of "interpretation" of the Constitution the Supreme Court has become a ruling oligarchy.[10]

Every culture is based upon some philosophy which provides a system of ground rules from which the major institutions—such as the political system—operate. "But," as media analyst Marshall McLuhan writes, "any change in the ground rules of culture nonetheless modifies the structures."[11]

The ground rules of American government have been altered. The old forms, such as the Constitution and representative government, remain but with different content by way of interpretation. This is dangerous because those who pull the strings of power have seized an arbitrary and capricious power while trumpeting the virtues of the old forms. Thus, the people are deceived.

The ramifications of the courts' usurpation of power are great. Robert H. Bork, a former Solicitor General, Yale law professor, and now a federal court of appeals judge, writes that the effects are threefold.

In the first place, "the area of judicial power will continually grow and the area of democratic choice will continually contract. We will have a great deal more constitutional law than the Constitution itself contains."[12]

Supreme Court and lower federal court judges are not elected officials but are appointed. Thus, the idea of representative government, especially on the federal level, has been eroded.

Consider this in light of the fact that among our constitutional freedoms or rights clearly given in the text of the Constitution "is the power to govern ourselves democratically."[13]

The second effect "will be the nationalization of moral values as state legislative choices are steadily displaced by federal judicial choices."[14] The diversity of moral and other choices which once characterized this country has steadily been made uniform. The obscenity and abortion decisions by the Supreme Court are examples of this effect. The Court, in opposition to both traditional moral standards and current public opinion, has set a legislative standard which the rest of the country *must,* by *force of law,* follow.

Third, there has occurred what Bork calls "the gentrification of the Constitution."[15] The constitutional gentry or elite— those who are not intimately involved with constitutional adjudication: federal judges, law professors, members of the media— will, Bork argues, continue to increase their control over the people. And they will decide issues according to *their* value systems.

Many now realize that Bork is correct in his analysis. They know very well that Supreme Court decisions, in general, do not emanate from the Constitution. Instead, they generally emanate from the Court's view of what constitutes good policy. This is legislating by the judiciary based on sociological jurisprudence. Thus, the people have lost faith in a once venerable institution.

One other area of misgovernment that merits discussion is the federal bureaucratic agencies. These agencies constitute a *permanent* form of government that essentially stays in power even when presidential administrations come and go.

These agencies promulgate thousands upon thousands of regulations each year which have the effect of law. However, under Article I of the Constitution, only Congress has the authority to make laws. This safeguard was written into the Constitution in order to ensure that only our *elected* representatives would be able to put laws into effect. The people could then hold these representatives responsible and accountable by the electoral process. Although bureaucratic regulation has been upheld by the courts as falling within constitutional guidelines, Congress' delegation of power to promulgate regulations is not permissible under the Constitution (if correctly interpreted).

This is not so with the bureaucracy, for the bureaucrat is not elected. The result has been the promulgation of a whole bevy of laws (what the bureaucratic agencies call "regulations") without benefit of the electoral process. Thus, the representative process has also been subverted at this level of government.

To support the massive and cumbersome bureaucracy in carrying forth its regulations, the federal government has begun overtaxing the American people. This has fostered a tax protest rebellion. The Internal Revenue Service has reacted with some oppressive tactics that have been less than welcomed by the people.[16] All this creates not only a distrust but in some instances an extremely apathetic attitude toward the political process.

The way Americans vote says much about our political destabilization. In 1976 and 1980 only 54 percent of those eligible voted. The number of people voting for the president and Congress continues to decline—from 62 percent for president in 1952 to 54 percent in 1976 and 1980—and from 42 percent for Congress in 1954 to 35 percent in 1978.

What does this tell us? Simply that people, in general, do not believe that the outcome of the election matters. Thus, since fewer people are voting, unconstitutionally broad government and unchecked bureaucracy will most likely continue.

The American people intuitively recognize that the government is representing their interests less and less. Congress, especially, has become in many ways a rubber stamp for the courts while resisting basic reforms proposed by the presidency.

There seems to be a deadlock in our republic. As one commentator has written, "Congress has become an obsolete institution with its members and their growing staffs spending almost all of their time running errands for constituents and special-interest groups."[17] Likewise, former Senator Adlai Stevenson recently said, "I recognize now that Congress does very little."[18]

The real danger in the public's loss of faith in our governmental system is that people desire the contrary. They want to have faith in their government and they want a government that takes action on the massive problems facing us—problems, unfortunately, often created by the government itself. In this respect, a 1979 CBS News poll found that 66 percent of those polled would support a leader who would bend the rules to get things done.[19] Amidst the chaos there is at least the threat that many

Americans would accept an authoritarian figure, party, or set of "new" ideas.

Loss of a War Which Strikes at the Heart of a Nation

According to Kevin Phillips, "nothing is so conducive to . . . spiritual anomie as a loss of a war which strikes at the heart of a nation's and a culture's self-esteem and faith in old verities."[20] Germany lost World War I in 1918. Until then the story of Prussia was one of unbroken geographic and military advance.

Two things happened to America in the late 1960s—the collapse of national confidence in the Vietnam War effort and in America's global role. This was referred to as the "trashing of America" by sociologist Robert Nisbet and writer Tom Wolfe.[21]

The Vietnam War and the reaction at home were related. Historically, any major war breeds great social change. The war and the defeat were a wound in America's pride.

The initial problem was not whether the war should be fought against communism, but how it should be fought—forcefully or anemically. Soon, the great majority of the public shifted to deny that America should resist communism at all, at least unless there was an invasion of our mainland.

The question remains as to how severe a wound that war was. Phillips notes:

> The American belief in Manifest Destiny, honed by centuries of westward advance from Manila Bay to V-J Day, was shaken during the 1970s much as Germany's self-image was after November 1918.[22]

Growing from this parallel is the idea of unilateral military disarmament. The present-day peace movement and the nuclear freeze people all have their roots in the Vietnam debacle.

There are some issues in the peace movement we can agree with. Nuclear war would be a nightmare. It would have been better if nuclear weapons had never been conceived. But they have been.

Reality tells us that if America weakens its military stand, then the Communist bloc will take advantage. One can see how in Afghanistan and Poland the Soviet Union thought it safe to oppress the people. Likewise, if the balance of power is destroyed, there is no doubt either militarily or politically that the greatly superior Soviet forces would overrun Western Europe, if not the United States.

We must be careful not to forget that the Communist bloc has a very low view of people. Sterling Segrave in *Yellow Rain* clearly documents that the Soviets have been using a horrible biological gas agent on a number of countries under their domination. The truly appalling thing that emerges from Segrave's book is the fact the Russians have tested and used those agents on their own countrymen.[23]

The materialists of the Communist bloc are tyrants and oppressors. With their low view of human life we cannot expect anything else. Oppression, therefore, is not incidental to their system; it is a logical necessity. Poland, the Gulag, and Stalin's purges should be an eternal reminder to this.

The peace movement, although well founded in some instances, is utopian in a fallen world. It could prove disastrous because the nuclear deterrent is the only barrier holding the Soviet forces from greater world domination and terror.

More importantly, for the moment, is the reflection the peace movement casts of the psyche of the American people. It is definitely another sign that we are a people who are unsure of ourselves.

This brings us to another question that some are asking: Do the American people even have the stamina to defend themselves? Would we surrender under the threat of nuclear blackmail by the Soviets?

In his controversial BBC interview in late 1975, Aleksandr Solzhenitsyn caused great concern in Great Britain when he said the moral consciousness of the West had descended so low that the Soviet Union did not need weapons to conquer the West. All it needed, he remarked, was its bare hands.

Modern Complexities

The parallels to Hitler and Stalin are definitely there, but with modern complexities. "Anyone who ignores the idea of some kindred underlying dynamics between the German political and cultural reaction to the 1920s and the emerging American reaction to the political and cultural trauma of the last two decades is . . . making a big mistake. The stimuli and pathologies are similar enough to warrant concern."[24]

However, there are important differences between pre-Nazi Germany and present-day America—differences which make the emergence of a Hitler-type leader even easier. The main difference may be the predominance of the electronic media in our country. Under the watchful eye of the television set, there is now a path of least resistance.

Two areas which have been subject to manipulation in recent years are those concerning religion (traditional values) and human life. Traditional value structures were the first great loss. Next to follow was the devaluation of human life through legalized abortion, incipient infanticide, and euthanasia. Both are ominous parallels to pre-Nazi Germany and the beginning of claims of total ownership by the state.

4 THE LOSS OF TRADITIONAL VALUES: THE RISE OF COSMIC SECULARISM

Whatever may have been the case in former times, we live today in a society characterized by ideological pluralism. Just as a shift occurred in the way people viewed religious values in the pre-Nazi German culture, there has also occurred a shift in thinking in American society.

The shift came slowly but increased in speed during the early 1900s. Before this time society operated from a set of presuppositions largely derived from the Christian ethic. These principles were generally guiding lights to those who drafted our founding documents and provided leadership in early America. This is not to say that a majority of Americans were ever Christians, but that the majority were *influenced* by Christian principles.

The Christian Memory

The breakdown of the Christian base cannot be underestimated in its effect on the present and future of America. As the memory of the Christian base that once provided a foundation for freedom has faded, the tendency has been toward centralized, authoritarian government.

The historical foundation for freedom was the belief in the Creator who established moral absolutes and gave to man absolute rights such as "life, liberty and the pursuit of happiness . . ." As the Declaration of Independence states: "That to secure these rights, governments are instituted among men."

To summarize, the Christian base included, first, the concept of man's createdness. Man was believed to be created in God's image and was to reflect God. Man then acquired, in a reflective manner, the characteristics of God. This afforded man great worth and dignity.

Second, rights were seen as an endowment from the Creator and, as a result, were absolute. Thus, rights were not products of the state. Government, then, could not legitimately take away what God gave and government had not given.

Third, the purpose of the state was to protect the God-given rights of men. As the Declaration proclaims, whenever a government systematically attacks or attempts to destroy these rights, "it is the right of the people to alter or abolish it."

This was the base for political freedom in America. However, when the freedoms we enjoy were separated from the Christian base, the distorted and perverted remnants became a force of destruction.

This was illustrated early by the French Revolution. Those who led the revolution in France in the late eighteenth century based much of their thinking on principles drawn from the Declaration, absent the Christian base. The result was a bloodbath and tyranny—a boot stamping on a human face.

We face that same possibility today. Many of those who lead the modern technological elite openly attack the Christian base. Many of those who lead the news media also do so.

A representative of the new secularistic ethic is Dr. Francis Crick. He is an avowed atheist who, along with James D. Watson, discovered the DNA code. In a speech Crick made in March of 1971 in St. Louis he said:

> [Y]ou must realize that much of the political thinking of this country is very difficult to justify biologically. It was valid to say in the period of the American Revolution, when people were oppressed by priests and kings, that all men were created equal. But it doesn't have biological validity. It may have some mystic validity in a religious context, but . . . [i]t's not only biologically not true, it's also biologically undesirable. . . . We all know, I think, or are beginning to realize, that the future is in our hands, that we can, to some extent, do what we want.

Harvard behaviorist B. F. Skinner clearly holds that man is nothing more than a cog in a machine. He writes: "Life, liberty, and the pursuit of happiness are basic rights. But they are the rights of the individual and were listed as such at a time when the literatures of freedom and dignity were concerned with the aggrandizement of the individual. They have only a minor bearing on the survival of a culture."[1]

If these comments were found in a comic strip we could laugh at them. But Crick and Skinner are giants of their times and when they speak, people listen to them. Their ideas and philosophy have consequences. Moreover, they speak for many other leaders of the technological elite.

Their philosophy is a complete repudiation of what the framers of the Declaration and the drafters of the Constitution believed. It means there is no Creator and that man has only relative rights. Also, the elite (those who control the state) administer government, not for the benefit of the governed, but to manipulate the country for their own ends. As Crick said, "we can do what we want"—that is, so to speak, they can play god.

"Unnatural Axe"

The predominant thought form undergirding the basic institutions of our society, especially since the 1930s, has been humanism.[2] Humanism, especially when it denigrates to materialistic secularism, not only drastically severs man's relationship to the Creator but lays a relativistic philosophical base.[3]

Under relativism the concepts of truth and nontruth become blurred. As a consequence, people, once they accept relativism, by definition cannot know what the truth is. Instead, they can only guess as to the best course to follow. Thus, it becomes easier to sell nontruth to such a society.

The blurring of truth and nontruth is well illustrated in pre-Nazi Germany. The bigger cities, like Berlin, were very much cabaret cultures. Berlin was known for its transvestites, the cocaine use of the famous, the abundance and easy access to pornography in all forms, and the contempt for the ordinary German citizen and German patriotism depicted in the cartoons of George Grosz and others. The comparative freedom of Germany in the 1920s gave rise to a flowering of new talent in the arts.

One example of the new talent was the Dadaists who in 1916 stated their purpose as cultivating the senseless by unleashing on the public every imaginable version of the unintelligible, the contradictory, the absurd. "Dadaism," said its advocates, "is against everything, even Dada."⁴ Thus, it was against every form of civilization and every form of art. It denied the existence of truth or beauty.

The Dada movement portrayed the meaninglessness of modern Western thought, art, morals, and traditions. Its spirit was one of anarchy and nihilism, seeking authentic reality through absurdity. Irrationality and chance were its guides. Even the movement's name was chosen at random by placing a finger in a French dictionary (*dada* is French for rocking chair).

"Art," the Dadaists said, "is sh--"—a dictum faithfully implemented by pictures of the Mona Lisa wearing a mustache, or by collages pieced together from the leavings in somebody's gutter, or by exhibits such as Max Ernst's in Germany in 1920. Leonard Peikoff writes:

> One entered the exhibit through a public urinal, in order to contemplate, among other items, a block of wood with a notice asking visitors to chop at it, an aquarium containing sundry objects immersed in a blood-colored fluid, and a young girl in a communion dress loudly reciting obscene poetry.⁵

Of course, this is extreme but no more extreme than watching the main character in the film *The Wall,* a major hit of 1982, squeeze a razor blade between his fingers and follow by shaving his eyebrows off and then the nipples on his chest, or seeing him floating in a swimming pool of blood.

What does it mean? These things are a weather vane which clearly shows which way the winds of culture are blowing: in the direction of undermining and invalidating the older values. There are no guideposts from which action can be judged. Anything goes.

"Our culture is breaking down," writes H. R. Rookmaaker in *Modern Art and the Death of a Culture,* "and if any confirmation is needed, go to the films, read the books of today, walk round a modern art gallery, listen to the music of our times."⁶

The music young people listen to today and accept is indeed a clear indication that a generation of youth is being spawned in a new irrational ideology. Contemporary rock music, as Rookmaaker notes, is "completely nonintellectual, with a thumping rhythm and shouting voices, each line and each beat full of angry insult to all Western values . . . their protest is in their music itself as well as in the words, for anyone who thinks that this is all cheap and no more than entertainment has never used his ears."[7]

Much of modern music, and in particular punk rock and new wave, bears a striking similarity to the Dadaism of the early twentieth century. As one observer noted:

> In London during the height of punk rock . . . I saw a massive exhibition of Dada and surrealism at the Hayward Gallery. The similarity between what was happening just across town was amazing. Dada and punk graphics were often practically indistinguishable. In context punk seemed like Dada taken to the streets. Which, in ways, it was.[8]

A certain class of punk rock music is aimed at instructing its listeners in a form of Nazi ideology. In fact, some working class and lower middle class teens in both Great Britain and the United States have been identifying with swastikas and the nihilism of punk rock music in a subtle form of racism.

This is seen even in small communities like McKenzie, Tennessee (which is characteristic of other areas of the country). There, in November 1982, it was discovered that a group of high school students were operating a Nazi cell group. Even though the grandfather of one of the students explained the cruelty of the Nazis under Hitler, the student said today's Nazi Party efforts are directed more at blacks than Jews. "That's the main thing I joined for," the student said, indicating that he "skips over" references to Jews in the Nazi literature he receives.[9]

In light of this, ponder the following lyrics from "Youth Corps," a song by Unnatural Axe, a punk rock band:

> We're apolitical, antihistorical
> We don't care about the past . . .
> We're movin' in for sure
> An Aryan culture takeover
> Lightnin' fast . . .
> Our thoughts are roarin'
> And there's no ignorin' the potential

In our minds . . .
We've got the idea
So you better hide dears
Hurry up there's no time,
We've arrived, we'll survive
We're the Youth Corps.[10]

This language represents another potential parallel—anti-Semitism. Anti-Semitism has dramatically increased in Europe. As *Newsweek* reports: "All across Western Europe, nasty incidents aimed at Jews are on the increase."[11] There are also signs of a resurgence of anti-Semitism in this country.[12]

The typical grass-root response to what was happening with the youth and in the arts in Germany and what is presently occurring in this country was a sense of outrage. In Hitler's case it created a political opportunity. For instance, Hitler first criticized and then banned modern art. His National Socialists replaced antiwar films with epics about Frederick the Great and called for a renewed German family, work, and the Fatherland.[13]

Such efforts in this country to censor art and literature merely strike at the symptoms of the moral disease. As such, it will have a very limited effect. Art and literature are simply antennae reflecting the culture and, in some instances, pointing the way toward the future. Unfortunately our antennae are telling us that trouble is ahead. And straightening the antennae without reforming the culture, as Hitler has shown us, cannot prevent the slide toward decadence.

Cosmic Secularism

Corresponding with the move away from traditional values is the move toward a technological society. This, along with the predominance of materialism in our country, has given us a secularistic culture.

Futurist John Naisbitt argues that with the coming of high technology there has also been a natural tendency for people to seek what he terms "high touch."[14] Naisbitt comments:

Perhaps the most powerful technological intrusion was television, far more vivid and more engaging than either radio or the telephone. At almost exactly the time we first introduced television, we created the group-therapy movement, which led to the personal growth movement, which in turn led to the human potential movement (est, TM, Rolfing, Yoga, Zen, and so forth—all very high touch). Television and the human potential movement developed almost in lockstep . . .[15]

In other words, human beings intuitively seek something beyond our society's machineness. Invariably, it is an attempt to touch something beyond man, a spiritual something.

Secularism cannot give the necessary spiritual side of life that man, an inherently religious being, needs. Thus, many Americans have entered the human potential movement. The concept that people can develop godlike capabilities, without the need of God, underlies this movement. This was the searching cry behind the remarkable 1982 movie *Blade Runner.*

The same thought is expressed in many forms of Eastern spirituality. It is not surprising for a leader in Eastern religion to proclaim: "The Buddhists and the Jains do not depend on God; but the whole force of their religion is directed to the great central truth in every religion: to evolve a God out of man."[16]

Strange as it may seem, this philosophy does not, in actuality, run contrary to secularism. As Brooks Alexander writes: "Secular humanism tries to define itself in opposition to the supernaturalism and 'irrationality' of all religions. But it actually operates on the basis of assumptions compatible with the aims of Eastern spirituality . . . Secular humanism regards humanity, both collectively and individually, as the source of meaning and value in life."[17]

Life thus has significance only in terms of man or his collective, mass humanity. This means that man is his own lawmaker—in effect, his own god. *Est's* Werner Erhard, a leader in the human potential movement, pushes the principle to its extreme in his summary of the *est* philosophy:

RULES ABOUT LIFE
by
Werner Erhard
1. Life has no
rules
2.

There is only one rule and one absolute: Life has no rules, except as determined by the individual.

Joseph Stalin held this same philosophy when he remarked that in order to make his omelette he would have to break a few eggs. By this he meant killing and maiming people and forcing them into concentration camps.

Proponents of secularism, because it fails to acknowledge the spiritual side of man, have in recent years begun dabbling with religion to fulfill the universal need, while denying its religious nature to avoid admitting a spiritual dimension. They do this by dabbling with elements of Eastern religion (such as Transcendental Meditation and astrology). Secularism, then, has become cosmic in that it has accepted some religious forms that do not threaten its own existence, while denying their religious nature.

An example of this is found in *Science Digest* in an article entitled "Boost Creativity—Stimulate Your Brain with Breath Control," in which the author extols Hindu yoga breathing techniques as a means of enhancing mental performance. Citing ancient Chinese, Egyptian, and Hindu sources, the author offers the observation that "controlled breathing may be the key to startling feats performed by yogis, from sleeping on nails to being buried alive."[18]

Secularism, then, cannot give true structure to man. Whether he believes it or not, man is a creature of God, and he will continually seek out structure for his inherent spirituality and religiousness.

This is one reason for the popularity of the cults. They offer that much needed structure. Unfortunately the structure offered is coercive.

The cults demand and create enormous discipline through forced labor, beatings, and their own ostracism or imprisonment. Psychiatrist H. A. S. Sukhdeo of the New Jersey School of Medicine, after interviewing survivors of the Jonestown mass suicide and reading the writings of members of the People's Temple, concludes: "Our society is so free and permissive, and people have so many options to choose from that they cannot make their own decisions effectively. They want others to make the decision and they will follow."[19]

Sherwin Harris, whose daughter and ex-wife were among the men and women who followed Jim Jones to death in Guyana, has summed up the dilemma: "This is an example of what some Americans will subject themselves to in order to bring some structure into our lives."[20]

Finally, most people today know very well that secularism leads to nowhere. That is why adults can sit in religious-oriented movies like *E.T.*, *Chariots of Fire*, and *Gandhi* and be emotionally moved.

This is true even if the audience finds the value system of the characters portrayed as repugnant. For example, the religious beliefs and practices of Eric Liddell, a Christian, in *Chariots of Fire* run totally contrary to our materialistic age. Yet many who, if they had met Liddell in real life would have been turned off, identified with his life in the movie. Although this is contradictory, it does illustrate the dilemma of modern man who, while having no faith in a personal God, yet longs for a spirituality that only the Creator can give.

Again, people are reaching out for the spiritual even if it is in the form of the mystical "Force" of George Lucas's *Star Wars* movies. To most, the Force is better than the nothingness of secularism. Unfortunately, the human need for a spiritual dimension is often met by cults or the occult.

The Occultic State

In an article in the *SCP Journal*, editor Brooks Alexander notes that as the fusion of secularism and Eastern religion continues, cosmic secularism will increasingly weave its ideology "into the fabric of Western thought and become more and more accepted as the usual way of looking at things."[21] Thus, cosmic secularism is deceptive. However, as we have seen, this is where recent art forms serve well as antennae of what is, in reality, happening.

The real danger in the emergence of cosmic secularism is not limited to its deceptiveness. It is in its acceptance by the organs of the state.

As Harvard professor Harvey Cox writes, secularism will use the organs of the state to perpetuate its ideology. It is, as he notes, "a closed system" and will actively oppose other religious systems.[22] We have seen this in the aggressive removal of certain aspects of Christianity from public places (such as public schools), as well as in the media's nearly systematic disparagement of Christians and Christian beliefs.

More dangerous, however, is that occultism is actually cosmic secularism taken to its logical conclusion.[23] Nazi Germany, a secular state, eventually slid into occultism. In his book *God and Beasts: Nazis and the Occult,* Dusty Skylar documents the occultic practices of those in leadership of the Nazi regime, from Hitler down.[24]

For at least three decades the Soviet Union, another militantly secular state, has financed many major studies in occult phenomena.[25] What kinds of studies are being financed? "Mind over matter (telekinesis), telepathy, and extrasensory perception. . . . Sight without eyes. Hypnosis-induced reincarnation. Precognition. Bioplasmic bodies (auras). Prophecy and astrology."[26]

What does this tell us? It gives us some idea of where American society and the American state may be heading.

The Christian Failure

Secularism is a dead end. It provides no basis for a belief in God or for man as a being with any worth or dignity. In the words of G. K. Chesterton: "When a man ceases to believe in God, he does not believe in nothing. He believes in anything."

This is exactly where modern Christianity has left our society. It has also left the church helpless before the modern state.

Again, it is important to take a lesson from history. Professor J. S. Conway in his study of the Nazi state writes that four factors may be held chiefly responsible for the churches' meager resistance to Hitler.

First was the ingrained tradition of pietism—a dichotomy between religious faith and the external world.[27]

This was due in part to the predominance of liberal theology and higher criticism that existed in pre-Nazi Germany. These tended to denigrate the authority of the Bible, thus making its relevance and application to the external world more difficult.

The tendency of many Christians to limit their religious loyalties to the narrow goal of personal redemption has undoubtedly led to sincere and devout lives. However, the failure to carry

their Christian principles into political and social life has opened
the way for control of the state by the proponents of secularism
and humanism, who have no such limitation on living their
"faith." Fortunately, the recent trend has been for more involvement of Christians in the political and moral issues of our times.[28]

Second, there was the German readiness to accept the existing political order without criticism and to exact obedience to the
state.[29] Conway writes:

> The illusions entertained by churchmen about their Nazi rulers,
> even after the horrifying consequences . . . and the overrunning of
> neighboring countries, can be explained—if not explained away—
> by the traditional acceptance that "the powers that be are ordained
> of God." The German Church was not equipped with the theol-
> ogy adequate to sustain any critical attack upon the actions of its
> political rulers, and for that reason, even at the end of the Nazi era
> there was no more than . . . a "reluctant resistance."[30]

With a recent surge of Christian activism and the publishing
of books on resistance, there has been a revival of interest in
"resistance" theology.[31] We can hope that these developments will
form the basis, if need be, for resistance to any tyrannous acts by
the state.

Third, some German churchmen threw in their lot with the
Nazis in the state's call for a renewal of the nation and a revival of
its spiritual life. Unlike the Protestant churches, the Catholic
Church committed itself to a policy of official opposition to the
Nazi party. The Catholic Students Union, however, is an example
of an endorsement of the Nazi effort. The Union issued the
following proclamation on July 15, 1933:

> The Catholic Students Union hails the National Socialist revolu-
> tion as the great spiritual breakthrough of our time. It is the
> destiny and the will of the Catholic Students Union to embody and
> disseminate the idea of the Third Reich . . . and therefore the
> Catholic Students Union will be led in the National Socialists
> spirit. . . . Only the powerful National Socialist state, rising out of
> the Revolution, can bring about for us the re-Christianization of
> our culture.
>   Long live the Catholic Students Union! Long live the
> Greater German Reich! Heil to our Führer, Adolf Hitler![32]

This type of rhetoric is a call for the state to do what the church would not do—that is, bring about a spiritual revival. By shifting their hopes for revival from the church to the state Christians were forced to closely identify with the state and German nationalism. This made it much easier for Hitler to manipulate the church.

Fourth, Conway writes that the churches' "basically conservative outlook . . . led them to accept without question the claim of Nazism to be the only alternative to communism."[33] In other words, because Nazism *appeared* to be conservative, the church leaned in its direction. However, because a philosophy is labeled conservative does not necessarily mean it is Christian.

For these basic reasons the German church, in general, failed to stem the Nazi tide. Through its lack of resistance the church became as silent as a tomb. It would not intermeddle, interfere, or protest acts of the state.

Those who oppose the truth desire a church which will not interfere. In Germany, Nazi Joseph Goebbels said: "Churchmen dabbling in politics should take note that their only task is to prepare for the world hereafter."[34]

Too many Christians have, albeit unknowingly, taken Goebbel's advice. "There is nothing," writes William Barclay, "that the world would like so much as a silent Church."[35]

The Cult of the State

A man will inevitably become like the god he worships. Much of the inhumanity that surrounds us today exists because modern man, in effect, has come to worship the secular state. As Jacques Ellul has written:

> What was lost by the church has been found by the [political] parties, at least those worthy of the name. Faith in attainable ends, in the improvement of the social order, in the establishment of a just and peaceful system—by political means—is a most profound, and undoubtedly new, characteristic in our society. . . . And this faith takes shape in active virtues that can only arouse the jealousy of Christians. Look how full of devotion they are, how full of the spirit of sacrifice, these passionate men who are obsessed with politics. . . . In this fashion a nation becomes a cult by virtue of the millions of dead who were sacrificed for it. It must be true, as so many agreed (did they?) to die for it.[36]

5 THE DEVALUATION OF HUMAN LIFE: THE FINAL PARALLEL

At one time no one would have thought that anything could exceed the horrors of the gas chambers in Nazi Germany or even the death camps of Stalin's Russia. However, the devaluation of human life in modern America has given us a parallel to the Auschwitz horrors that surpasses anything that has come before them, both numerically and in cruelty to the victims.

The April 1982 decision of an Indiana court allowing a six-day-old infant to be starved to death because of congenital problems raised with clarity the question of the sanctity of human life in this country. The judge in that case reasoned the parents could lawfully refuse to feed "Infant Doe," which led to a certain death by starvation. Infanticide, once unthinkable, burst into the open and became thinkable—a reality.

This is illustrated by a *Newsweek* feature article on infanticide that appeared only six months following the demise of Infant Doe. The article discusses infanticide in animals and, without any credible evidence to sustain the conclusion, ended by inferring that infanticide was a logical aspect of human behavior.

> [I]nfanticide can no longer be called "abnormal." It is, instead, as "normal" as parenting instincts, sex drives and self-defense—and every other behavior that lets an animal [human beings] save a little piece of itself from death by passing its genes into the next generation.[1]

Note the evolutionary premise: man is just an animal. A total callousness toward human life (abortion, infanticide, and euthanasia) has become part of our cultural heritage. One tragic example of this is the death several years ago of a fourteen-year-old girl, Marcy Renee Conrad of Milpitas, California.

Marcy Conrad had been raped, strangled to death, and left lying off the road in the hills outside town. At least thirteen students went out to look at her body. One girl picked up the murdered girl's jeans, cut off a patch, and threw the jeans down along the side of the road. One student tried to cover the body with leaves. Another took his eight-year-old brother along to see the body. One boy went twice. Those who saw the body went back to class or to the pinball arcade. One went home to bed. Another student said he only cared about collecting the marijuana cigarette he had won on a bet that the body was real. As one local newspaper reported:

> The shock is the shock of the encounter with icy indifference, the indifference of the kids in the first instance, but, much more importantly, of the culture that produced them. . . . The depersonalization did not begin yesterday; it is not unique to this moment, yet it seems more complete—and they seem more alienated and isolated—than what we have ever known before.[2]

A Will-to-Death

Sigmund Freud, the father of modern psychology, theorized that the will-to-death (what he called the "mortido instinct") is the basic and governing fact in the lives of all men. Accordingly, Freud had dim hopes for the future of human civilization.

Many years before Freud, Solomon in Proverbs 8:36 stated the position of the Creator that "all they that hate me love death." Thus, theologically there is a will-to-death in those who stand in opposition to the Creator.

This brings us to an important point. It is not simply that modern men hate life, but that they hate the Creator. Every person and every infant in the womb is in the image of God and possesses the resulting dignity given by the Creator. When the abortionist kills an unborn baby he is in reality killing the image of God. Although abortionists make the argument that the unborn infant is not a person, their position is, in actuality, based upon the nonexistence of any image of God or dignity of prenatal life—because of the nonexistence of God and the nonoccurrence of creation.

This is man in total rebellion against his Creator. The ultimate result of the rebellion is death—even a love of death.

The love of death is very prominent in the prodeath movement. The love of death is a cultural and personal fact. When men do not love the Creator, they will not love their fellowman. There is, then, an inextricable link between respect toward God and respect for human life. Once the cord is cut between God and man, man can be nothing more than a product of the evolutionary chain and no different from any other evolutionary product—that is, an animal.

Modern materialistic science cannot understand man because it does not understand the Creator. Modern science is materialistic in that it sees nothing beyond matter. As Francis Crick has written: "As soon as we understand cell chemistry, we know that a metaphysical explanation of life becomes superfluous."[3]

Man has been reduced by modern science to a chemical reaction. This is the view of man that Dr. A. E. Wilder-Smith writes "is taught avidly and dogmatically, indeed universally, in most schools and high schools."[4]

As a chemical reaction, man then is no different than any other matter. He is junk and a throwaway.

Because of this degradation of man and the dignity of human life, we are facing a modern holocaust. To understand our place in history, a brief look at the decline toward the sanctity of life that led to the German holocaust is instructive.

The Prelude to the Holocaust

Under the Weimar Republic in Germany, in spite of great pressure from certain intellectual quarters, abortion remained illegal. However, the laxity of the German courts, especially in those areas where Christian influence was weak, made the practice of abortion fairly common in pre-Nazi Germany.

This, along with the economic depression of the 1920s, caused a sharp decline in the German birthrate, so that German population growth had virtually stopped by 1933.

Hitler realized that in order for Germany to become a dominant economic and military power, its population would have to increase. Thus, he pragmatically tightened enforcement of the antiabortion laws and introduced other measures to spur population growth, just as the Soviet Union is presently doing even though abortion remains legal.

These population growth policies, however, applied only to what was considered *genetically sound German families*. For the non-Aryan groups within the Third Reich—Jews, Poles, Gypsies, and Czechs—there was a contrary policy.

In his trial at Nuremburg, Dr. Helmut Poppendick, chief physician of the Main Race and Settlement Office under Hitler, explained:

> [T]he Nazi racial policy was twofold in aspect, one policy being positive and the other negative in character. The positive policy included . . . the encouragement of German families to produce more children. The negative policy concerned the sterilization and extermination of non-Aryans, as well as other measures to reduce the non-Aryan population.[5]

Among those other measures was abortion. Thus, after the war the War Crimes Tribunal indicted ten Nazi leaders for "encouraging and compelling abortions," which it considered a "crime against humanity."[6]

In America, abortion has been presented as the only sure means of reducing the birthrate and averting the highly propagandized threat of overpopulation. Herein lies the difference between the American and Nazi endorsement of abortion. The Nazis relied first upon sterilization, and later upon euthanasia/extermination as the primary vehicles for eliminating excess population, resorting to abortion only as a subsidiary tool. They had the technical advantage of a totalitarian regime which could act without regard of public opinion. However, as attorney Michael Schwartz writes:

> The American population controllers had a somewhat more difficult task of enticing the people to inflict these crimes upon themselves. They had to sell convenience, the advantages, even the necessity of abortion as their primary vehicle of population reduction, while sterilization and euthanasia, at least so far, have been auxiliary tools in the fight against life. This difference in tactics is merely accidental.[7]

The greater powers in shaping American policy with regard to population control and abortion are groups such as Planned Parenthood, Zero Population Growth and the Population Institute. These organizations grew out of the eugenics movement, which flowered in the 1920s.

Eugenics is the science and art of improving human breeds by applying the principles of genetics and inheritance to secure a desirable combination of physical characteristics and mental traits in a selected race of people. The eugenics movement, which is obviously racist at core, grew out of a felt need by a certain social and academic elite to keep the American white race pure—an elite, by the way, which still exerts a prominent influence on our society and government.

American eugenists, for example, were instrumental in attaining a restrictive immigration law passed in 1924 that eliminated most immigration into this country from Eastern and Southern Europe.[8] They also were instrumental in getting compulsory sterilization laws passed in a majority of the states during those years. In fact, the law for the Prevention of Progeny with Hereditary Disease, the basis of Hitler's race purification program, was directly patterned on the model sterilization law proposed by the leaders of the American eugenics movement.[9]

Therefore, the prodeath mentality which begins with an acceptance of abortion can eventually lead to the extermination of whole classes of people, or to what the Nazis called the "final solution." However, could America travel the road of Nazi Germany? A realistic appraisal of certain key factors indicates that we are already well along the way.[10]

Depersonalization of the Victims

A theme repeated by the Nazis was that the Germans were dealing with a variety of racial groups, most of whom were designated as inferior. Those not of the Aryan physical quality desired by Hitler, as he said, "had to be treated like tuberculosis bacilli, with which a healthy body may become infested. This was not cruel, if one remembers that even innocent creatures of nature, such as hares and deer, have to be killed, so that no harm is caused by them."[11]

The Third Reich was in debt to the earlier theorists of Social Darwinism who asserted that social usefulness, pragmatically speaking, was a better guide for government and law than the untenable notion of human rights. The unfit and weak, then, should be either barred from marriage or sterilized.

This ideology is reminiscent of Francis Crick's position of the untenableness of the Declaration of Independence's proclamation of man's createdness and dignity. However, this prodeath philosophy found its expression early in American history in the form of a Supreme Court decision.

In 1927 Justice Oliver Wendell Holmes, Jr., delivered the Supreme Court's decision upholding the Virginia sterilization law in *Buck v. Bell*.[12] Carrie Buck, a young mother with a child of allegedly feeble mind, had scored a mental age of nine on the Stanford-Binet intelligence test. Carrie Buck's mother, then fifty-two, had tested at mental age seven. In one of the most famous and chilling statements of our century Holmes wrote:

> We have seen more than once that the public welfare may call upon the best citizens for their lives. It would be strange if it could not call upon those who already sap the strength of the state for these lesser sacrifices. . . . Three generations of imbeciles are enough.[13]

Recognizable in Holmes' statement are both pragmatism and collectivism. His low view of man is also apparent. As Holmes once remarked: "I see no reason for attributing to man a significance different in kind from that which belongs to a baboon or a grain of sand."[14]

Harvard professor Stephen Jay Gould writes that *"Buck v. Bell* is a signpost of history."[15] Likewise, Gould was "shocked" by an item in the *Washington Post* on February 23, 1980, wherein the headline read "Over 7,500 sterilized in Virginia."[16] The law that Holmes upheld was implemented for forty-eight years, from 1924 to 1972. The operations had been performed in mental health facilities, primarily upon men and women considered feeble-minded and antisocial—including "unwed mothers, prostitutes, petty criminals and children with disciplinary problems."[17]

Hitler, however, asserted that one "vermin" (the Jew) in particular had to be eradicated. Most simply, Hitler asserted that "the Jew is no German." He later labeled the Jew as a nonperson, thus depersonalizing an entire race of people.

Roe v. Wade, the 1973 Supreme Court decision legalizing

abortion, was another signpost of history.[18] The Court held that unborn children are not persons protected by the United States Constitution. The Court, in essence, placed the unborn child in the category of nonperson and what it called mere "potential life" that may be killed ("terminated").

From this premise there has been a systematic effort to dehumanize and depersonalize the being which abortion eliminates. Language especially has been used very effectively to distort the truth concerning abortion.

James Tunstead Burtchaell, for example, provides us with a list of dehumanizing linguistic phrases. The unborn has been designated as "protoplasmic rubbish," "a gobbet of meat protruding from a human womb" (Philip Wylie); "a child-to-be" (Glanville Williams); "the fetal-placental unit" (A. I. Csapo); "gametic materials," "fallopian and uterine cell matter" (Joseph Fletcher); "a part of the mother" (Justice Oliver Wendell Holmes, Jr.); "a part of the mother's body" (Thomas Szasz); "unwanted fetal tissue" (Ellen Frankfort); "the products of pregnancy" or "the product of conception" (Department of Health, Education and Welfare); "sub-human non-personhood" (F. Raymond Marks); a "child Who-Might-Have-Been" (James Kidd); "so much garbage" (Peter Stanley); "defective life," "the pregnancy" (Family Planning Perspectives); "live human material"; "a collection of cells"; "the conception" (Malcolm Potts); "potential life" (Justice Harry Blackmun); "a chunk of tissue"; "the fertilized ovum" (Sarah Weddington, attorney who argued for legalized abortion before the Supreme Court in *Roe v. Wade*).[19]

Abortionists do not talk about "babies" in the womb. They prefer to call them "fetuses." This semantic manipulation is used to completely dehumanize the unborn child. The child thus ceases to have a personality, and its destruction cannot possibly mean killing.

We must not forget that the idea that abortion is not killing *is a new idea.* Before 1973, the consensus was that abortion was killing, even in antiquity. Semantics, however, have done away with our conscience.

This fact is seen in the research conducted by Finnish researcher Dr. Martti Kekomaki. One nurse who observed Dr. Kekomaki's experiments on live aborted "fetuses" said:

They [the doctors] took the fetus and cut its belly open. They said they wanted its liver. They carried the baby out of the incubator and it was still alive. It was a boy. It had a complete body, with hands, feet, mouth and ears. It was even secreting urine.[20]

The baby was not injected with an anesthetic when doctors sliced his belly open. Asked to explain the implications of his research, Dr. Kekomaki said, "An aborted baby is just garbage."[21]

The total depersonalization of unborn children is also seen in the "model" eugenics program conducted at University Hospitals by the Wisconsin Clinical Eugenics Center of the University of Wisconsin (at Madison), which is a major Midwest center for late-term abortions. As I write these words, this institution offers parents the opportunity to view, fondle, and take home photographs of the handicapped children they have aborted.[22] Dr. Renata Laxova, director of the Center, writes:

> Parents are asked if they wish to see, hold the fetus (frequently they do), and whether they wish to receive photographs as well as copies of the autopsy report. After discharge, communication is maintained with the couple and their physician. An attempt is made to provide and ensure support during the grieving process.[23]

The "fetus," as Dr. Laxova refers to the unborn child, is without personality and thus, semantically speaking, the child is a nonperson.

The media has served as an indispensable ally to those who desire the dissemination of the dehumanizing semantics to a vast audience. A considerable segment of the media in contemporary America, while outwardly autonomous, is as much a tool for antilife propaganda as was the media of Nazi Germany.

Today's gatekeepers of information show no reluctance about depicting in frank fashion, with overt condemnation, the slaughter of baby seals or the threatened existence of the snail darter. However, when it comes to coverage of the slaughter of unborn children, a double standard of morality sets in. News that would shed a negative light on abortion is seldom printed and never are pictures of aborted babies printed—despite the fact that this is touted as the "right to know" age. In fact, the vast majority of the media echoes the distorted versions of those who are doing the killing.

Closely related to semantics manipulation is the use of euphemisms. To avoid all open mention of death, the Nazis in their official documents developed an elaborate, almost elegant euphemy. A partial glossary of Nazi extermination was "evacuation; resettlement; cleared of Jews; cleansing; disinfection; special treatment; labor in the East; injected off; put to sleep; discharge certificates; clean-up of the Jewish question; final solution to the Jewish question."[24]

There was the 1933 German Law for the Prevention of Progeny with Hereditary Disease (which effected prevention through sterilization or death); the Reich Committee for Children (which destroyed them); the Research Committee for Research on Hereditary Diseases and Constitutional Susceptibility to Severe Diseases (which identified those to be eliminated); the Non-Profit Patient Transport Corporation (which conveyed them to the clinics where they would die); the Charitable Foundation for Institutional Care (which paid for it); and there was "euthanasia" and "mercy death."[25]

Throughout the literature of the Nazi state, the theme of "favor" is repeated. The destruction of mentally or physically defective persons was called "an act of grace" and the "privilege of a mercy death." When it was later agreed at a conference called by Adolf Eichmann that "mongrel Jews" were to be offered their choice of deportation or sterilization, it was anticipated that "sterilization should be considered a favor and should impress people as such."[26] This was, in essence, Justice Holmes's reasoning in *Buck v. Bell.*

This is the same type of mentality that led to the *Infant Doe* case. The parents, the hospital, and the courts involved were "merely doing the baby a favor," in their semantically sanitized atrocities.

There are institutions in the United States that offer this kind of "favor." For instance, in Pittsburgh there is Women's Health Services, where the services have little or nothing to do with women's health. In Florida there is the Orlando Birthing Center, which will handle second-trimester abortions but no births. In Leiden one finds the Center for Human Reproduction, which is concerned to arrest reproduction, as also is the Water Tower Reproductive Center in Chicago. In Missouri, Parents Aid assists women to avoid being parents while in Chicago, Family

Guidance counsels people on how to prevent families. Pre-Term in Cleveland and Pre-Birth in Chicago preclude full-term births.[27]

The aim of the prodeath campaign is the same as the Nazi state. It is to allow for the unborn child's destruction without alarming anyone ordinarily concerned about human rights. To our shame, this campaign has in large part succeeded.

Abrogation of Responsibility

Another theme that echoes from the Nazi death camps is the denial of individual responsibility. The killings were attributed to the group or the collective.

James Tunstead Burtchaell writes that the philosophy was "for each person to account for his killing work by pointing out that he acted under the law, having submitted his judgment to those empowered to make decisions of state."[28]

In 1973 in *Roe v. Wade,* the Supreme Court, as an agency of the federal state, claimed that it would take no position on the question of when human life begins. The justices asserted that they withheld both ethical judgment and legal protection. However, "immediately after the Court had restrained itself from taking a moral stand, its legal decision began to be used as a reliable moral premise."[29] And in fact, the Supreme Court *did* take a firm position on when human life begins—that it does *not* begin at conception or during the first two-thirds of the unborn child's existence.

I used the following example in *The Second American Revolution,* but it bears repeating.[30] Six months after the decision in *Roe v. Wade,* Dr. Peter A. J. Adam, an associate professor of pediatrics at Case Western Reserve University, reported to the American Pediatric Research Society on research he and his associates had conducted on twelve babies (up to twenty weeks old) who had been born alive by hysterotomy abortion.

These men took the tiny babies and cut off their heads— decapitated the babies and cannulated the internal carotid arteries (that is, a tube was placed in the main artery feeding the brain). They kept the diminutive heads alive, much as the Russians kept the dogs' heads alive in the 1950s. Take note of Dr. Adam's retort to criticism:

> Once society's declared the fetus dead, and abrogated its rights, I don't see any ethical problem. . . . Whose rights are we going to protect, once we've decided the fetus won't live?[31]

Dr. Adam passed on responsibility to the collective. In this case, it was society. However, society's sanction came from the state in the form of a Supreme Court case.

This same lack of responsibility was exhibited in some of the testimony at the hearings held in January 1982 by the President's Commission for the Study of Ethical Problems in Medicine and Biomedical and Behavioral Research. The commission conducted hearings on the moral dilemmas posed by treating severely ill and handicapped patients.

Mary Anne Warren, a philosophy professor from San Francisco State University who specializes in medical ethics, testified that handicapped infants should have the right to die "painlessly."[32] Although Warren said some of her colleagues would wince at the analogy, she compared such a child to a horse with a broken leg.[33]

At the same hearing, Dr. Norman Fost, a pediatrician from the University of Wisconsin, also testified. He said a recent survey showed that 70 percent of his colleagues would accede to parental wishes that a deformed child not be treated, but allowed to die by starvation.[34]

Likewise, in June 1982 at a Yale-New Haven Hospital Symposium, Dr. Paul B. Besson, an expert in geriatrics, said there is a growing tendency in hospitals across the country to put "do not resuscitate" orders on charts of many elderly. "One notes a growing tendency to write orders saying do not resuscitate," he said. "We must never lose sight of the risk that this practice can put us on a slippery slope leading toward inhumane practices."[35]

Denial of individual responsibility in the past has led to a callousness toward human life. However, few of those who exterminated people for the Nazi state were purposely evil. As James Tunstead Burtchaell writes:

> There was Karl Brandt, chief of both the "euthanasia" and prison experiment programs, who as a young doctor had made plans to join Albert Schweitzer in his mission hospital work in Lambaréné. And there was Karl Gebhardt, of the castration and sterilization

project, who also worked on surgical techniques to rehabilitate handicaps of birth and injury. The monstrous work of these men seems not to have made them bestial off-duty or in the course of their usual human relationships.[36]

Likewise, the guards in the German extermination camps conditioned themselves to accept the atrocities. There was a divesting of self or responsibility.

Many had to struggle, however, with the occurrences at the camps. These events included major surgery being performed on prisoners by trained physicians "without the slightest reason," and without anesthesia, or an inmate being thrown for punishment into "a large kettle of boiling water, intended for preparing coffee for the camp. The [victim] was scalded to death, but the coffee was prepared from the water all the same"; or youngsters being picked out at random, "seized by their feet and dashed against tree trunks."[37]

One survivor of the camps reported that he saw flames "leaping up from a ditch, gigantic flames. [The Nazis] were burning something. A lorry drew up at the pit and delivered its load— little children. Babies! Yes, I saw it—saw it with my own eyes. . . . Was I awake? I could not believe it."[38]

Many of the guards conducting the massacre of children were fathers themselves. Their individual responsibility and guilt, however, had been passed to the state.

Many of those involved in the abortion movement have developed similar mentalities. For example, Dr. Howard Diamond of Beth Israel Medical Center in commenting on abortion has said: "Cultural—it's all cultural. Like eating snake meat. If you tell yourself it's disgusting, you'll get sick."[39] Or take Dr. William Rashbaum, veteran of thousands of abortions, who had for years suffered during each abortion removal the fantasy of the unborn child resisting, clinging to the uterine walls, fighting to stay inside. When asked how he managed to endure this fantasy, he remarked: "Learned to live with it. Like people in concentration camps."[40]

Not only the physicians but women who have abortions have lost any meaning of what it means to carry a child. For minimal reasons, unborn children are sacrificed to the abortionist's knife. For example, 53 percent of women interviewed at a

New York "health clinic" cited financial reasons as the most important element in their decision to have an abortion.[41]

Killing Is Big Business

Let us not forget that abortion is big business. The destruction of millions in Nazi Germany was a huge enterprise that depended upon cooperation from government, industry, the economy, and other societal institutions. A prime example of corporate profits was the I. G. Farben Chemical Corporation which sold poisonous gases and lethal drugs to the death camps for experimental and destructive purposes.

By the time abortion was legalized in this country in 1973, the decline in the birthrate had already caused concern among obstetricians. Abortion became a way to make up for lost revenue by doctors.

Dr. Bernard Nathanson, a co-founder along with Betty Friedan of the National Abortion Rights Action League and later author of *Aborting America*,[42] in a speech in Albany, New York, on March 17, 1981 remarked:

> There are 1.3 million abortions done in the United States at an average cost of $350.00 per abortion. That is an industry, ladies and gentlemen, of five hundred million dollars a year which [could be] ranked in the top ten of Fortune magazine's industries. It is enough probably to float the Chrysler Corporation for a year. I submit to you that allowing an elite like the medical profession with a substantial vested interest economically in this industry to make decisions about it, is the supreme conflict of interest.[43]

(After years as a proabortion activist, Dr. Nathanson came to understand the sordid nature of abortion and now opposes it.)

One doctor in Chicago alone billed Medicaid $792,266 for abortions in 1974 (and this only for his welfare customers).[44] One large abortion center promised a prospective abortionist in a recruitment letter: "Salary and fringe benefits will be extremely attractive. Imagine the opportunity to make at least $80,000 a year for no more than ten hours work each week."[45]

The half-billion dollar profit (or more) each year from the abortion industry affords it strong impetus to lobby against any restriction over abortion-on-demand. Likewise, the abortion industry gives financial support to activist organizations that work

toward that end. Moreover, many abortionist physicians participate actively in groups such as Planned Parenthood, the Religious
Coalition for Abortion Rights, and similar organizations. Yet little
is said of this vested interest in the media or otherwise.

The magnitude of the callousness of the modern age is
depicted in the commercial uses of unborn children. For example, in April 1980 guards at the Swiss-French border intercepted a
truck coming from central Europe, loaded with frozen human
fetuses destined for the laboratories of French cosmetic factories.
In a French newspaper it was explained that there is a brisk trade
in fetal remains for "beauty products used in rejuvenating the
skin, sold in France at high prices."[46]

American pharmaceutical and chemical companies have a
strong interest in fetal materials. Since there are at least 1.6
million abortions a year, these materials are relatively abundant.

Evidently employees at the District of Columbia General
Hospital did not have any qualms about selling the organs of dead
babies. In 1976 the *Washington Post* broke a story on how the
hospital's pathology department had collected more than $68,000
from commercial firms for organs removed from stillborn and
dead premature babies.

The head of D. C. General's obstetrics department acknowledged that some of the baby organs came from "late-term elective
abortions."[47] He said the money earned from these sales went to a
special fund for equipment, a television set, expenses for sending
physicians to conventions, and to buy soft drinks and cookies for
visiting professors.[48]

For years, there have been accounts of the traffic in fetal
material from foreign countries to a United States military instal-
lation in Maryland, where fetal organs were used in medical
studies.[49]

Newsday once reported that an Ohio medical research company tested the brains, hearts, and other vital organs of 100 fetuses as part of a $300,000 pesticide research contract for the
Environmental Protection Agency.[50]

There have also been published reports about a Chicago
firm which advertised the sale of human embryos and other
organs encased in "paperweight" novelty items.[51]

Is this not the same mentality that pervaded the Nazi concentration camps? The use of unborn babies for cosmetic products is precisely like the Nazi use of Jewish remains to make soap. The leap from elective abortions to fetal experiments to cosmetics to entombed embryos in paperweights to lamp shades made from human skin (as the Nazis did) is not that far a jump.

The Pain of the Hidden Victim

Just as the Nazis concealed extermination of their victims from the public, so the abortionists take elaborate measures to ensure that attention is not focused on their victims. Advanced technologies conceal the victims and dispatch them into oblivion in a bureaucratic, ultra-efficient, assembly-line manner. Seldom do we ever see an aborted child. An exception occurred in Los Angeles in February 1982 when 500 fetuses were found packed in jars of formaldehyde behind the home of the proprietor of a medical laboratory—some apparently third trimester abortions.[52]

Those who support *Roe v. Wade* are committed to the idea that a fetus, being only "potential life," cannot feel pain, pain being an attribute of actual life. Evidence, however, now indicates that unborn children do experience pain—especially in light of the gruesome abortion methods.

There are four principal means of abortion. Sharp curettage involves a knife killing of the unborn child. Suction curettage involves a pump which sucks out the child in pieces (and a knife cleans out any remnants). These methods are primarily used in first trimester abortions.

In second trimester and later abortions, a saline solution (referred to as "salting out") is injected into the amniotic fluid. The salt acts as a poison. The skin of the unborn child, when delivered dead, resembles skin soaked in acid. If by accident the solution leaks into the body of the mother, she experiences pain that is described as severe. The unborn child can suffer in this solution for two hours before its heart stops beating.

Alternatively, the mother can be given a dosage of a chemical sufficient to impair circulation and cardiac functioning of the unborn child, which will be delivered dead or dying.

There are uncertainties about the precise points in fetal development at which particular kinds of sensations are experienced. But observations of development and behavior indicate that by the fifty-sixth day an unborn child can move. Discomfort may occasion this movement. Tactile stimulation of the mouth produces reflex action about day fifty-nine or sixty. By day seventy-seven the unborn child develops sensitivity to touch on hands, feet, and genital and anal areas, and begins to swallow. In other words, by the seventy-seventh day an unborn child in many ways would feel the same sensations we would, including pain.

George F. Will writing in the *Washington Post* notes: "Americans are proud of their humane feelings and are moved by empathy. Thus, we regulate the ways animals can be killed. Certain kinds of traps are banned. Cattle cannot be slaughtered in ways deemed careless about pain. Stray dogs and cats must be killed in certain ways. . . . But no laws regulate the suffering of the aborted."[53]

If fetal pain is acknowledged, America has a problem: its easy conscience about 1.6 million abortions a year depends on the supposition that such pain is impossible. America simply ignores the medical evidence of the pain to avoid the problem. Thus, we are faced with the same callousness as exhibited by those in Hitler's Germany who piled the babies in ditches and watched them burn.

The Invisible Church

The legal and medical professions have been virtually silent in the face of the abortion holocaust. Long since departed from its ethical mooring, these professions by their silence are as guilty as the abortionists.

The courts have even gone so far as to uphold the right of parents to money damages for "wrongful births." For example, the Virginia Supreme Court in 1982 held that a couple could collect $178,000 because a hospital laboratory, apparently through error in labeling test results, failed to inform them their unborn daughter could be born with a fatal hereditary disease. The parents said they would have aborted the child if they had known she would be born with disease.[54]

The legal profession is now cultivating the idea that women stand a much lower chance of dying after a legal abortion than they do after giving birth. To the contrary, "the risk of a healthy woman's dying from elective abortion is extremely rare," reported an article in the *Journal of the American Medical Association*.[55]

These things are occurring without moral comment. The ethical silence is appalling.

Particularly troubling has been the silence of the Christian community in the face of the human life issue. Again there is a German parallel.

The lack of resistance of the Christian churches to the Nazi state's Jewish policies has been the concern of extensive and still unconcluded literature. The Nazis noticed early that the churches took their stand, not on the issue of human rights of all Jews, but on an expedient and self-serving concern for "Christian Jews." The church by its expediency and lack of political involvement was eventually neutralized by the state.

Sadly, the same thing has happened in the United States. The American churches and the Christian community have been amply alerted to abortion as the primary issue facing the country today through the books, films, and work of the prolife movement. Still, very little in the way of true resistance to the wanton slaughter of human life is coming from Christianity.

In all this one principle must be understood: Although the church may cry for religious freedom from here to eternity, a state that will not protect human life ultimately will not protect freedom of any kind. Instead, such a state will systematically attack freedom until the only freedom left is the "freedom" to die.

6 THE DECLINE OF THE FAMILY

A book on the "liberated" view of lesbianism[1] was reviewed by the *New York Times* several years ago.[2] The review noted that although lesbianism had been a burden to the women's movement, this book would change all that. In particular, the book would assist in overcoming "the nuclear family, that cradle of evil."[3]

To scorn and attack the traditional family unit is not new. What is new is the breadth and depth of the attack in the United States, a country once thought to be family-oriented. Unfortunately, as Cornell University professor Urie Bronfenbrenner has pointed out, "The family is not currently a social unit we value or support."[4]

As a consequence of such open attack and deemphasis, the family unit in American life has unquestionably suffered. In addition, the social fabric which is being torn is to a large extent a result of "the deteriorating family life and the conditions that undermine declining care for our children."[5]

The decline of the traditional family unit has been accompanied by the transference of functions once administered by the family (such as education, health, and welfare services) to other institutions, primarily the state. The family, which is "a critically important institution in shaping our children's minds, values, and behavior,"[6] has become in many instances a mere extension of the state.

Many have voiced their concern over the crisis in the American family. Little, however, has been done to emphasize the need for a return to a family-oriented society. On the contrary, many government agencies, including the courts, have not only undermined the family but have endorsed programs and policies antagonistic to the traditional family unit.

Decline in Family Structures

In the past thirty years the change in family structure has been dramatic. Nine major trends unfortunately indicate that the "traditional nuclear family . . . seems unlikely to return any time soon."[7]

First, there has been a sharp decrease in traditional family households. Alvin Toffler writes:

> If we define the nuclear family as a working husband, a housekeeping wife, and two children, and ask how many Americans actually still live in this type of family, the answer is astonishing: 7 percent of the total United States population. Ninety-three percent of the population do not fit this ideal . . . model any longer.[8]

The shift away from the traditional family means that most families no longer conform to the traditional stereotype of a husband being the sole wage-earner for his wife and children. It also means, as Stanford University sociologist Lenore Weitzman notes, that "the *variety* of family and nonfamily households has increased so that many more Americans will have several different types of family experiences (such as divorce and remarriage) and will live in different types of family households (such as single-parent households and remarried 'blended families') at different points in their lives."[9]

These "new" family models (including a generation of day-care "orphans") will be with us for a long time, and American families will grow even more "diverse." That is the conclusion of a report by demographers at the Joint Center for Urban Studies of MIT and Harvard University.[10]

Second, there has been a historic decline in the birthrate over the past 200 years. As we move toward zero population growth, women today not only want fewer children, but they are also delaying pregnancy. As a result, a large percentage of young married couples are childless. As Professor Weitzman writes:

In 1970, 45 percent of the married couples with a husband under 25 did not have children. By 1980 the percentage rose to 52 percent. Childless couples with a husband aged 30-34 rose from 10 percent in 1970 to 18 percent in 1980.[11]

The rapid rise in abortion from 22,000 in 1969 to more than 1.6 million in 1982 has also added to the childless home phenomenon.[12] The availability of contraceptives has also contributed to the phenomenon. For example, in "1960 only one couple in ten who did not want to have a child was using the pill, the IUD or sterilization. The proportion rose to one-half of the couples by 1970, and to three-fourths by 1975."[13]

Third, for the first time in this century it has become more probable that any single marriage will end in divorce than that the marriage will last. Our current divorce rate is annually the highest in U.S. history. There are now more than one million divorces a year (1,210,000 in 1981). There "is every indication that the rate will continue at a very high level."[14]

Current projections by the United States National Center for Health Statistics suggest that approximately 50 percent of the current marriages will end in divorce. However, as professor Weitzman cautions, "even this projection may be too conservative because it is based on the experience of past generations."[15]

One major effect of the high divorce rate has been the vast number of children affected by the trauma of divorce—ultimately the children of more than half the existing marriages. For example, "in 1954 there were 341,000 children under the age of 18 in divorcing families; by 1975 the number had increased to 1,123,000."[16] As University of Chicago law professor Franklin Zimring says, "What's happening to the kids is just a howling shame."[17]

According to current statistics, it can be said without reservation that a high divorce rate will remain a predictable feature of American society. A major factor in predicting a continuing high divorce rate lies in women's increased participation in the labor force and independent earnings. For example, "women with higher salaries in 1968 were more likely to have separated or divorced by 1972."[18] (Another factor is lax divorce laws and the emergence of no-fault divorce.)

Fourth, there is a trend toward remarriage and the formation of "new" families through a life cycle. A strikingly high proportion of divorced people remarry—over 80 percent.[19]

Fifth, the high divorce rate and the longer time between divorce and remarriage have contributed to the increase in single-parent families. In fact, between "1970 and 1980 single-parent families increased by 52.3 percent."[20] Single-parent families now comprise 13 percent of all U.S. households.[21]

The result has been that one in five children under eighteen in America today lives in a single-parent family.[22] About 19 percent of families with children (over double that for black families) are now headed by a single parent.[23] It is projected that by 1990 the proportion of children living with one parent will increase to 25 percent.[24]

Sixth, the sharp, sustained increase of employment of married women over the past three decades is one of the most profound changes in American family patterns. The statistics tell the story:

> In 1890, less than 5 percent of all American wives worked outside the home for wages and salaries. By 1940 this figure had increased to 17 percent, but the most dramatic increases followed World War II. In 1947, 20 percent or one out of every five married women was employed in the labor force. The proportion rose to one in four (25 percent) by 1950, one in three (32 percent) by 1960, and to one out of two (48 percent) by 1980.[25]

Economist Ralph Smith forecasts that by 1990, 67 percent of all wives—two out of every three—will be in the labor force.[26]

Seventh, another major change in the labor force participation of married women has been the increase in the number of employed *mothers.* Between 1940 and 1978, the labor force participation rate of mothers with children under age eighteen showed a phenomenal 500 percent increase, from 9 percent to 50 percent. In fact, in 1978 more than half (58 percent) of all American mothers of school-age children were in the labor force.[27]

More surprising is the number of employed mothers with children under age six. In 1950 only one out of ten wives with preschool children were in the labor force. By 1960 the proportion had risen to one out of five. By 1970 it was close to one out of three. In 1980 the proportion, at 45 percent, was rapidly approaching one out of every two.[28]

In addition, even women with children under three years of age are entering the labor force in large numbers. By 1975, 33 percent of all mothers with children under three were employed—twice the 1960 rate.[29]

Eighth, recent years have brought a decline in the perceived legitimacy of male authority within the family. "We have moved," Professor Weitzman writes, "from the belief that the male should be head of the family to the ideology that egalitarian arrangements are best."[30]

A major thrust in the direction of egalitarian family patterns is coming from women's increasing dissatisfaction with the traditional roles of wife, housekeeper, and mother. The changing ideological position of the women's liberation movement has created strong pressures for change in the role of women in the family. The demands have been for greater independence and compensation in the labor force by women. In fact, as Professor Weitzman notes, the movement of women into the labor force may "be viewed as both a cause and an effect of changes within the family."[31]

Ninth, recent years have seen a steady increase in the number of single people of the opposite sex who are living together in nonmarital cohabitation. The number of cohabiting couples grew dramatically from 523,000 in 1970 to about 1,500,000 in 1980. The actual number of unmarried couples is, according to Weitzman, probably close to three million couples or six million adults.[32] As a result, the last decade witnessed a sharp rise in births to unmarried women, including the "explosion" of teenage pregnancies, not to mention the increased use of contraceptives by unmarried women.[33] The last decade has also included a sharp increase in abortions by unmarried women.

As the traditional family fades, the vacuum it leaves is being filled with what Alvin Toffler calls "a bewildering array of family forms: homosexual marriages, communes, groups of elderly people banding together to share expenses (and sometimes sex), tribal grouping among certain ethnic minorities, and many other forms coexist as never before."[34]

Consequences

There are many ill consequences that flow from the breakdown of the family. One inevitable consequence is the growth of the state and particularly its role in family matters.

Traditionally, the family has served as a buffer zone between the individual and the state. With the decline of the family the logical consequence has been the governmental bureaucracies and the massive state school systems—in effect, a "brave new world" type of all-encompassing "health and human services" welfare state.

As parents have abrogated their responsibility toward the family (by way of divorce and otherwise), they have also inadvertently transferred their rights and responsibilities of parenthood to the state. And the state has proven to be a poor substitute family.

A dire consequence of the family's breakdown has been alienation and loneliness. As Toffler writes, "We are witnessing a population of 'solos'—people who live alone, outside a family altogether. . . . Today, a fifth of all households in the United States consists of a person living alone."[35] These individuals are the young who have not yet married, the elderly, and the growing ranks of the newly divorced.

John Naisbitt is correct when he states "that the basic building block of society is now the individual rather than the family."[36] The buffer is fading, and we find more and more that we are standing naked against the state.

The total effects of the women's liberation movement have yet to be fully evaluated. One certain effect has been the redefining of the woman's role in the home, as well as her relationship to her husband and her children (if any), and the state's assumption of the functions of the traditional mother.

As women have moved into the work force, their role outside the home has also been redefined. The feminists view women in the work force as a key to their movement. An interview in *Working Women* magazine of nine top corporate women revealed their belief that the basic method of breaking male dominance in the business world is having more women in the work force.

This raised a question of what to do with children of working mothers. The answer was state-financed day-care centers.[37]

This is an invitation for the state to assume another family function—rearing small children.

Instead of being the cradle of future generations, modern women, in large part, have been reduced to sexual parity with men. The concept that women belong to a higher estate than men has waned significantly in recent years. George Gilder writes: "They must relinquish their sexual superiority, psychologically disconnect their wombs, and adopt the short-circuited copulatory sexuality of males."[38] Women, once the center of the home, are now, in many instances, the receptacles of male sexual frustrations.

And now, if unplanned pregnancy does result from sexual union, the abortion avenue is increasingly open. Abortion essentially legalizes murder in the life of the family at the sole choice of the "mother." Indeed, the womb of life has often become the cradle of death.

The sad consequence of the fading family is the breakdown in traditional parent-child relationships and the destructive impact this has had on American youth. A generation has now grown up in the nonfamilial era, and they no longer know how to relate personally or in a family context.

In fact, parents have lost the ability to interact with their children. As Professor Urie Bronfenbrenner writes:

> Our study of middle-class fathers of one-year-old infants found that they spent an average of only 20 minutes a day with their babies. When a recording microphone was attached to each infant's shirt, the data indicated that in terms of true, intimate interaction between father and child the average daily time together was *38 seconds.* One survey I did of the child rearing practices in the United States over the past 25 years reveals a decrease in all spheres of interaction between parents and their children.[39]

The result, as recent surveys indicate, is that at every age level children today show a greater dependency on their age-mates than they did ten years ago. Gone are the vertical relationships of parent and child. They have been replaced by the horizontal relationships of peers.

The horizontal peer relationships for years have been an

integral part of the socialization process of the public schools. As a consequence, there has been a move away from parental relationships to peer relationships along with all the trappings of "peer pressure."[40]

Compulsory public education produces a peer group that occupies a place of primary importance in the life of the student. As James Coleman has noted:

> This setting-apart of our children in schools—which take on ever more functions, ever more "extracurricular activities"—for an ever larger period of training has a singular impact on the child of the high-school age. He is "cut-off" from the rest of society, forced inward toward his own age group, made to carry out his whole social life with others his own age. With his fellows, he comes to constitute a small society, one that has most of its important interactions *within* itself, and maintains only a few threads of connection with the outside adult society.[41]

In essence, this means that the primary relationship is not parent-child or, for that matter, it is not even child-child. Instead, it is child-state in that the parental vacuum has been filled by the state-controlled public education system. Indeed, as some tell us, a primary function of public education is to provide for a "uniform orientation at the societal level."[42]

This means that human relationships at every level have broken down. Thus, the alienation and confusion that so characterize modern man have left him easy prey for control.

It must not be forgotten that the dictators who have ruled the totalitarian states of the twentieth century have not been self-confident men. They have been weak men. However, they know how to prey on weakness, uncertainty, and fear. As history shows, in an age of self-doubt and alienation an authoritarian leader often rises to the top.

The Disappearance of Childhood

The greatest consequence of the family's decline may be the loss of childhood. Over the past several decades we have rapidly moved toward what Toffler calls a "child-free culture."[43]

As I write, twelve- and thirteen-year-old girls are among the highest-paid models in America. In many advertisements in the visual media, children are presented to the public in the guise of knowing and sexually enticing adults through eroticism and soft-core pornography.

In cities and towns throughout the country, the difference between adult crime and child crime is rapidly narrowing. For example, in the year 1950, in all of America, only 170 persons under the age of fifteen were arrested for what the FBI calls serious crimes (such as murders, forcible rape, robbery, and aggravated assault).[44] Statistically, this means that in 1950, adults (defined as those over and including fifteen years of age) committed serious crimes at a rate 215 times that of child crime.

By 1960, in just ten years, youth crime had soared. By that time adults committed serious crimes at a rate 8 times that of child crime. By 1979, the rate was 5.5 times.

Does this mean that adult crime is decreasing? To the contrary, adult crime is increasing, so that in 1979 more than 400,000 adults were arrested for serious crimes.[45] In fact, between 1950 and 1979 the rate of adult crime increased threefold.

The rise in child crime, however, was staggering. Between 1950 and 1979, the rate of serious crime committed by children increased 11,000 percent! The rate of less serious child crimes (such as burglary, larceny, and auto theft) increased 8,300 percent.[46]

The rise in child crime has initiated a move toward eliminating the distinctions in punishment between children and adults. This is reflected in a new series of state laws. For example, in New York children between the ages of thirteen and fifteen who are charged with serious crimes can now be tried in adult courts and, if convicted, can receive long prison terms.[47]

The distinctions between adults and children are clearly breaking down. In his important book *The Disappearance of Childhood*, New York University professor Neil Postman argues convincingly that the media has eradicated any such distinctions.

Postman argues that in the Middle Ages (or what some historians term the "Dark Ages") "there were no children" in the sense that children were treated differently than adults.[48] Children worked at very early ages and shared in the same entertainment and activities as adults. In fact, it was common for children to be present at even ribald events, and fondling the genitals of children was not an uncommon form of entertainment.

It wasn't until the early 1800s with the humanitarian move to treat children differently, especially in the form of protective legislation, that children developed into a different class. From that time, what has traditionally been called childhood has been with us up to the mid-twentieth century.

Postman sees 1950 as a watershed year in the decline of childhood. He remarks:

> I choose 1950 because by that year television had become firmly installed in American homes. . . . It is in television . . . that we can see most clearly how and why the historic basis for a dividing line between childhood and adulthood is being unmistakably eroded.[49]

First of all, the accessibility of information that television provides breaks down adult-child distinctions. As child psychologist David Elkind writes in *The Hurried Child:* "Television, by simplifying information access, has opened up for children areas of information that were once reserved for adults."[50]

All the doors to the adult world that were once closed to children are now open through the windows of the television set. As Postman states: "The essential point is that TV presents information in a form that is undifferentiated in its accessibility, and this means that television does not need to make distinctions between the categories of 'child' and 'adult.' "[51]

Most children have unlimited access to television. For example, one study indicates that three million children (age two to eleven) are watching television every night of the year between 11:00 P.M. and 11:30 P.M.; 2.1 million are watching between 11:30 P.M. and midnight; 1.1 million between 12:30 A.M. and 1:00 A.M.; and just under 750,000 between 1:00 A.M. and 1:30 A.M.[52]

Television offers a very primitive form of communication— pictures. It is primitive in that watching television requires no skills and develops no skills.

The television image is available to everyone, regardless of age. The programs, commercials, and products are not just for three-year-olds. As Postman sees it:

So far as symbolic form is concerned, *Laverne & Shirley* is as simple to grasp as *Sesame Street;* a McDonald's commercial as simple to grasp as a Xerox commercial. Which is why, in truth, there is no such thing on TV as children's programming. Everything is for everybody.[53]

Because of pressure by advertisers, television has zeroed in on the eighteen-to-forty-nine-year-old audience almost to the exclusion of all others.[54] For example, even ten years ago there were a number of programs that included young children and, occasionally, their problems in the series. Examples are *The Brady Bunch, The Courtship of Eddie's Father,* and others.

Contrast these shows with those current today in which there are few children in the traditional sense, contemporary series such as *Happy Days, Laverne and Shirley,* or even *Different Strokes.* The talented young man in *Different Strokes* is much advanced beyond his years and is not a child in the traditional sense.

With the exception of a few children's shows and cartoons, even young children consistently end up watching programs geared for adults. In these programs children are exposed to the issues and conflicts of adults as if they were adult viewers.

Television also keeps the entire population in a condition of high sexual excitement. It stresses, as Postman notes, "a kind of egalitarianism of sexual fulfillment; sex is transformed from a dark and profound adult mystery to a product that is available to everyone—let us say, like mouthwash or underarm deodorant."[55]

One obvious consequence of this has been the rise in teenage pregnancy. Although not caused exclusively by salacious television, television has doubtless been a powerful factor. Births to teen-agers constituted 19 percent of all births in America in 1975, an increase of 2 percent over the figure in 1966. But if one focuses on the childbearing rate among those age fifteen to seventeen, one finds that *"this is the only age group whose rate of childbearing increased in those years, and it increased 21.7 percent."*[56]

Grimmer statistics show that the consequences of adultlike sexual activity among children has steadily increased the extent to which youth are afflicted with venereal disease.[57] As Postman notes, the "traditional restraints against youthful sexual activity cannot have great force in a society that does not, in fact, make a binding distinction between childhood and adulthood."[58]

Alcoholism, once considered an exclusively adult addiction, now looms as a reality for children. Of other drugs, such as marijuana, cocaine and heroin, the evidence is conclusive. American youth consume as much of these as do adults.[59]

There are other massive indications that we are losing childhood and that the adult-child distinctions are disappearing.[60] One such indication is the "child's rights" movement, which rejects adult supervision and control of children and provides a philosophy to justify the dissolution of not only parenthood but also childhood. Professor Postman writes:

> [The child's rights movement] argues that the social category of "children" is in itself an oppressive idea and that everything must be done to free the young from its restrictions. This view is, in fact, a much older one than the first, for its origins may be found in the Dark and Middle Ages when there were no "children" in the modern sense.[61]

The old restraints are being unplugged. Civilization, however, cannot exist without the control of the impulses of the young, particularly the impulse toward aggression and immediate gratification.[62] "We are," as Postman forecasts, "in constant danger of being possessed by barbarism, of being overrun by violence, promiscuity, instinct, egoism."[63]

As in the Middle Ages, the explicit use of children as a means for the satisfaction of adult sexual fantasies has already become acceptable. This is being conditioned by the use of children as erotic objects on television and in movies.

The Cradle of Evil?

Childhood is definitely fading. We are also at a point where children are not only unnecessary (abortion is a clue to this), but the elderly are also. Margaret Mead writes: "I believe this crisis in faith can be attributed . . . to the fact that there are now no elders who know more than the young themselves about what the young are experiencing."[64]

If there are no elders, there is obviously no need for the hierarchical structure of the traditional family which depends on authority. Thus, the family may be slowly sliding into obsolescence. And once again the state (and its agencies)—by default—has gained influence over an area of life once unfettered by government interference.

The anarchy from this situation is tellingly illustrated by the statistics set forth in this chapter—an anarchy that could very well be ordered by some form of authoritarianism.

As the interest groups and state agencies invade and interfere with those who want to keep the traditional aspects of the family intact, one can expect little protection from the courts. In fact, the courts have provided the fodder for those who would see the traditional family removed altogether from American life.

7 JUDICIAL SCHIZOPHRENIA: THE COURTS AND THE FAMILY

A person suffering from schizophrenia is one possessing a split personality—that is, two personalities within one person. In recent years the governmental and legal systems have exhibited a schizophrenic attitude in their positions on the family.

The Supreme Court, it appears, has suffered from an acute case of this disease. In the fashion of Orwellian doublespeak, the Court has on the one hand praised the traditional family while on the other it has systematically chopped at the roots of this most basic institution.

With its decisions having the full authority of law, the Court's pronouncements on the family have had a tremendous, but negative, impact on the family. This has resulted in a course by the state which, if not altered, will irreparably damage the family.

Sexual Privacy and the Family

In the early history of this country the courts, especially the Supreme Court, upheld the sanctity of the traditional family.[1] Beginning in the early 1970s, however, the Supreme Court launched a new line of cases that marked a sharp break from the past.

For example, in *Eisenstadt v. Baird* the Court extended *unmarried* persons the right to determine the appropriate use of contraceptives.[2] The significance of this decision has been noted by at least one legal scholar:

[H]istorically the Court had upheld the marital institution in glowing terms which followed the traditional Christian explanation. But *Eisenstadt* completely failed the traditional test since no such right had ever been found in the "rooted traditions" of the American people.[3]

The logic of *Eisenstadt* flows inexorably into the abortion decision of *Roe v. Wade*. "The right to abortion was founded on the right to privacy which was said to be located in the ninth or fourteenth amendments. But more importantly, no distinction was made between the unmarried plaintiff, Jane Roe, and the married plaintiff, Mary Doe."[4]

Underlying these decisions as defined through the right to privacy was the idea that people have a *right to choose* certain lifestyles or modes of expression even in the context of the family. Thus, the "choice" of the individual takes preference even if exercised within the family and even if it is detrimental to the stability of the traditional family unit.

In the 1973 decision of *Roe v. Wade* the Court elevated, in the name of a so-called constitutional right of privacy,[5] a woman's right to "mental health" above the life of an unborn child in her womb. In the first six months of pregnancy,[6] the woman was granted a constitutional right to abortion if upon consultation with her physician it was decided that her health would be jeopardized by having the baby.[7] The life of the unborn child was, in effect, subordinated to the woman's *convenience*. The essence of *Roe* is that abortion cannot be forbidden at any stage of pregnancy. Thus the Court, in essence, approved abortion-on-demand.[8]

In 1976 in *Planned Parenthood v. Danforth* the Court ruled unconstitutional a Missouri statute that required the husband's consent before a married women could obtain an abortion.[9] The statute obviously reinforced the traditional family role of the husband as head of the wife and of the household. The Court, however, ruled that the state could not constitutionally reinforce that family structure to the detriment of the wife's right of choice.

In *Danforth* Justice Blackmun disregarded both the family's existence independent of the power of the state and the husband's interest in the unborn child as a party in the impregnation process. Blackmun dismissed the Missouri statute as follows:

> Clearly, since the State cannot regulate or proscribe abortion during the first stage . . . the State cannot delegate authority to any particular person, even the spouse, to prevent abortion during that same period. . . .
>
> The obvious fact is that when the wife and the husband disagree on this decision, the view of only one of the two marriage partners can prevail. Since it is the woman who physically bears the child and who is the more directly and immediately affected by the pregnancy, as between the two, the balance weighs in her favor.[10]

The interest of the husband as the head of the household and as the father of the unborn child was again subordinated to the woman's convenience.

In the *Danforth* case, the Court also ruled unconstitutional a Missouri statute which required written consent of a parent or guardian for an unmarried woman under the age of eighteen to obtain an abortion during the first trimester of pregnancy. Again, the Court endorsed a constitutional principle diametrically opposed to traditional family autonomy.

In *Danforth,* a lower district court had previously upheld the parental consent provision because it found "a compelling basis . . . in the State's interest 'in safeguarding the authority of the family relationship.' "[11] In disagreement Blackmun stated: "Any independent interest the parent may have in the termination of the minor daughter's pregnancy is no more weighty than the right of privacy of the competent minor mature enough to have become pregnant."[12] The interest of the parents to control the upbringing of their minor daughter was thus subordinated to their daughter's convenience.

In the area of abortion, then, the Court has created the autonomous wife and the autonomous child to the detriment of the traditional family structure. The implications of the abortion decisions are ominous for the family in other areas.

For example, the Court has extended the principle of child autonomy beyond abortion. In a 1977 decision the Court held unconstitutional a state statute which restricted the sale of contraceptives to those over sixteen years of age, and then only by a licensed pharmacist.[13] Such a statute runs contrary to the right of privacy of minors, the Court said.

In response to this newly declared right, the United States Court of Appeals for the Sixth Circuit held that minors possess a right of privacy which includes the right to obtain contraceptives without having to consult their parents. Although acknowledging that parents are interested in contraceptives being distributed to their children, the court held that the state may not require a family planning center to notify the parents concerned.[14]

In *H. L. Matheson,* the Supreme Court did uphold the constitutionality of a Utah statute which requires a physician to "notify, if possible" the parents of a dependent, unmarried minor girl prior to performing an abortion.[15] This decision is narrow and appears to reduce parents to the level of state-employed consultants.

Freedom Against Parental Authority

This new liberty for children from parental control over their sexual lives rests upon a much broader principle than the right of privacy.

An early warning signal was sounded in the 1960s in *Tinker v. Des Moines Independent School District.*[16] While this was a lawsuit brought by parents on behalf of their children, the Court laid the framework for other constitutional rights that children would later assert in opposition to their parents.

In *Tinker* high school students wore black arm bands in protest of the Vietnam War to school. The students were disciplined by school authorities and suit was brought.

Writing for the Court in *Tinker,* Justice Fortas stated that students "in school as well as out of school are 'persons' under our Constitution. They are possessed of fundamental rights which the State must respect."[17] Public schools, that had so long stood *in loco parentis* (or in place of the parents) to their students, had now become a public forum for free speech activities even if parents objected. This means that students have the constitutional right to do in public schools (over parental objection) what parents may conceivably prohibit at home.

If the *Tinker* rationale is transferred to the family unit, the implication is clear; the right to resist school authorities is, in essence, the right to resist parental authority. Similarly, is the family a free speech forum for all family members, including children?

Justice Hugo Black in his dissent in *Tinker* expressed great concern over the implications of the decision:

> [I]f the time has come when pupils of state-supported schools, kindergartens, grammar schools, or high schools can defy and flout orders of school officials to keep their minds on their own schoolwork, it is the beginning of a new revolutionary era of permissiveness in this country fostered by the judiciary. The next logical step, it appears to me, would be to hold unconstitutional laws that bar pupils under 21 and 18 from voting or from being elected members of the boards of education. . . . The original idea of schools, which I do not believe is yet abandoned as worthless or out of date, was that children had not yet reached the point of experience and wisdom which enabled them to reach all of their elders.[18]

Six years later Justice Lewis Powell expressed a similar concern in his dissent in another case.[19] The Supreme Court in this case held that students facing temporary disciplinary suspensions from a public school are entitled to such due process protections as prior notice and an opportunity for a hearing.[20] Powell said:

> [T]he Court ignores the experience of mankind as well as the long history of our law, recognizing that there *are* differences which must be accommodated in determining the rights and duties of children as compared with those of adults. Examples of this distinction abound in our law: in contracts, in torts, in criminal law and procedure, in criminal sanctions and rehabilitation, and in the right to vote and to hold office. Until today, and except in the special context of the First Amendment issue in *Tinker,* the educational rights of children and teen-agers in the elementary and secondary schools have not been analogized to the rights of adults or to those accorded college students. Even with respect to the First Amendment, the rights of children have not been regarded as "co-extensive with those of adults."[21]

The parallel between the public school cases and the *Danforth* case is a remarkable one. In *Danforth* the Court declared that "[c]onstitutional rights do not mature and come into being magically only when one attains the state-defining age of majority [when a minor legally becomes an adult]. Minors, as well as adults, are protected by the Constitution and possess constitutional rights," including the right to obtain contraceptives.[22]

This is not to say that children should not possess rights. Nor is it to say that children should not be protected, especially in the area of child abuse and related atrocities.

However, as Neil Postman previously observed, the mentality as exhibited by the Supreme Court effectively does away with childhood in the traditional sense. It also lays waste the family.

The *Danforth* rationale, law professor Bruce Hafen writes, "carried to its logical conclusion of extending 'fundamental' rights to children, carries serious implications."[23] Specifically, Hafen notes:

> [T]he uncritical application of egalitarian theory to children places them and their parents on the same plane in their relationship to the state. This apparently subtle shift has the enormous effect of removing parents from a "line position" between the state and their children, which not only exposes families to the risks of direct state access to children, but which raises basic new questions about the nature of parental responsibility. . . . For one thing, the state could revoke or limit its delegation, and in no case could "parents" exercise greater authority than could the state.[24]

There is yet another disturbing implication of Justice Blackmun's opinion in *Danforth*. The Court's "view reflects a surprising insensitivity to the distinction between public and private action generally and to the private authority of parents in particular. It also seems to assume that state support for parental authority falls automatically into the category of 'state action' for Fourteenth Amendment purposes."[25] The consequence is that the Fourteenth Amendment requirements of due process and equal protection (which in the past only applied to state action and not private action) gives antiparental rights to children.

In speaking of the "right to personal autonomy . . . autonomy which is particularly important for young people in their developmental stage,"[26] a writer for the *University of Pennsylvania Law Review* and an advocate for child's rights states: "The first amendment is premised on a belief that regimentation of mind and spirit block the advancement of knowledge and the discovery of truth; state regulation or *state-sanctioned parental interference* that intrudes on areas of belief and puts undue restrictions on spiritual development is inimical to these important developmental values."[27]

To some, then, any state sanction of parental control over children becomes, in effect, a violation of a child's rights. Therefore, in such instances state enforcement of these rights comes into play.

The family buffer, thus, may have dissipated. An illustration of the extent to which it has dissipated is found in *In re Snyder*[28] and some of its progeny.[29]

In *Snyder* a fifteen-year-old girl who was antagonistic toward her parents asked a juvenile court to declare her "incorrigible" and place her in a foster home. The girl had no police record and thus there was no evidence that she was incorrigible in the traditional meaning of the term. She had lived all her life with her natural parents in a typical middle-class family.

In an early phase of the case, the parents had been found to be "fit" parents in the statutory sense. The family had experienced friction because of differences of opinion between the parents and the girl concerning her dating, her friends, and her desire to smoke.

The court involved framed the issue as "whether there is substantial evidence to support a finding that the parent-child relationship had dissipated to the point where parental control is lost and, therefore, Cynthia is incorrigible."[30] Finding "a total collapse" in the parent-child relationship, the Supreme Court of Washington ruled the girl incorrigible.[31]

Snyder implies that a dissatisfied child has the right, as any adult would, to leave the family at her own request. Evidently it was Cynthia Snyder's decision that she preferred not to be subject to the authority of her parents, and her choice was upheld. *Snyder* is, therefore, an argument for the proposition that a child can "divorce," or at least achieve separation from, his or her parents on grounds of incompatibility.[32]

Who Owns the Child?

Early in 1923 the Supreme Court held: "The child is not the mere creature of the State; those who nurture him and direct his destiny have the right, coupled with the high duty, to recognize and prepare him for additional obligations."[33] Has the court come full circle since this decision when it was presupposed that the child is not the "mere creature" of the state?

Recent decisions of the Supreme Court seem to indicate that the family is no longer the basic institution for determining values for children. Instead, that is the state's province in and through its various agencies—in particular, the state-supported public schools.

With the rise of the child rights movement, the integrity of the family is threatened. One legal commentator writes that new "constitutional liberties possessed by children are, at least in part, rights that children can exercise *independently of their parents* and that cannot be delegated in a way that gives parents an arbitrary veto over these rights."[34]

Harvard law professor Laurence Tribe argues that when the parents "threaten the autonomous growth and expression of [family] members [i.e., children] . . ." then there is no longer any reason to protect family authority.[35] Who, however, is going to exercise the authority to determine when children are threatened by the family? The state, of course.

In light of the abortion and contraceptive cases, the old right of the parents to assume authority over their children has been lost. If parents cannot prevent their children from killing their offspring (who are the parents' grandchildren), then what is left? What parental decision could be more important? Surely, parents are to be more than consultants (contrary to the suggestions of the Supreme Court) to their children or information-gatherers for abortion clinics.

It must not be overlooked that the courts are agencies of the state. This means that they, too, are political institutions. As political institutions, they are driven somewhat by political motives.

Those who sit on the courts once sat in law schools that have discarded the Christian base that once undergirded law in the United States. This has given the courts a free hand in shaping the law. Working from an evolutionary base, the courts have, in effect, become shapers of social fabric rather than merely decision-makers.[36]

The family, like all other institutions, has been seen through the lens of social evolution. It, with the individual, is evolving. Should we then be surprised at the disturbing pronouncements of the courts?

The present judicial schizophrenia is the product of a lingering Christian memory in conflict with the predominance of secularism in our major societal institutions. The Christian memory affects even the courts in that the courts sense the loss of something vital (for example, the integrity of the family unit), but their presuppositions drive them to a logical conclusion; namely, that the individual autonomy should prevail over family autonomy. Even the difference between marriage and nonmarriage has been obliterated.

With the rise of abortion, infanticide, euthanasia, and the numerous liberation movements, and the reaffirmation of these practices in the courts, we have moved perilously close to the edge. And the Supreme Court's affirmative pronouncements on the family should not catch us off-guard. Indeed, such schizophrenia should alarm us.

In fact, Big Brother or Big Sister may be closer than most think. As George Orwell wrote in his futuristic novel:

> The family could not actually be abolished, and, indeed, people were encouraged to be fond of their children in almost the old-fashioned way. The children, on the other hand, were systematically turned against their parents and taught to spy on them and report their deviation. The family had become in effect an extension of the Thought Police. It was a device by means of which everyone could be surrounded night and day by informers who knew him intimately.[37]

To avoid the type of terror Orwell writes of, it is imperative that the courts and other state agencies remove themselves from tampering with the family. If not, there may be little hope for a free future.

8 THE CONFLICT IN EDUCATION

Two streams of conflict are confronting Christians in the present educational matrix.

First, free speech is restricted for Christians and other religious people in the public schools. Although the courts have held that public schools are forums for free speech purposes, religious speech has, in large part, been curtailed by overt discrimination.

Two examples come to mind. Several years ago near Albany, New York, high school students sought to hold a voluntary prayer session in their classrooms before the start of the school day. Federal judge Irving R. Kaufman outlawed the practice as "too dangerous to permit."

More recently in Lubbock, Texas, a high school board passed a regulation allowing students to meet before the school day to discuss, among other things, ethical and religious issues. This regulation was knocked down by a federal court of appeals as unconstitutional. Unfortunately, in January of 1983 the United States Supreme Court refused to review this decision.

Second, the rise of private schools, especially Christian schools, has threatened the state-supported public education monolith. With the proliferation of private schools and home school programs, the legal and political confrontations between state educational organizations and private schools have increased dramatically over the past decade. The issue has invariably been the state's attempts to regulate or control private schools.

Free speech in the public arena and freedom to operate private schools without state interference, therefore, are the two pressing issues in education today.

Public education has unfortunately become an instrument

of government policy. Through the courts the social engineers, in concert with various interest groups, have been able to use the government schools as instruments of social change. This should not surprise us since governments have long considered public education their most important tool for indoctrinating and controlling the young.

We have become so accustomed to public education that we have forgotten that the system that preceded it served us very well. As educator Samuel Blumenfeld writes, "The truth is that the system that prevailed prior to the introduction of compulsory public education was not only quite adequate for the young nation, but served the public need far better than anything we have today."[1]

The Early Schools

America began its remarkable history without public education—with the exception of some local common schools in New England. The federal Constitution does not even mention education, and it certainly does not enumerate a federal power to aid or regulate education. From the beginning of this country, education was an area of concern left to the families and churches in the individual states. At that time, education was almost exclusively private, although it was often financially aided by the state.

This was a consequence of the close relationship that existed between the church, the school, and the family in early America. As Blumenfeld writes, "American intellectual history is inseparable from its religious history."[2]

Not only did the colonial experience with education, both public and private, rest upon a close connection between church and state, but so did the early efforts to broaden private schools in the states by added financial aid after the American Revolution. In all but one of the thirteen states, the people were taxed by the state to support the preaching of the gospel and to build churches.

After the Revolution there was some disestablishment of the Anglican Church, but none of the states in the eighteenth century, by their constitutions, prohibited the state from financing religious activities. This included the building of churches and the maintenance of pastors. In addition, many of the states had established churches or Protestant religions.[3]

It was not until 1853 that the Massachusetts Constitution was amended to include a provision ending tax support for schools operated by a religious sect. Even as late as 1919 there was a close link between the public school and religion in Massachusetts. In fact, tax money could be used to support public and private schools so long as "no denominational doctrine is included."[4]

As a consequence of the strong Christian influence on early American culture, the schools in their curriculum and methods were dominated by Christian ethics. That influence was so strong that Christian theism was predominant in education, both public and private, throughout the nineteenth century. For example, the New England Primer in colonial America opened with certain Christian admonitions followed by the Lord's Prayer, the Apostles' Creed, the Ten Commandments, and the names of the books of the Bible.

Education and, in particular, education in religion remained a high priority throughout early American history. For example, the Northwest Ordinance of 1787, which set aside federal property in the territory for schools and was passed again by Congress in 1789 (the same Congress that wrote the Constitution) states the purpose of those schools: "Religion, morality, and knowledge being necessary to good government and the happiness of mankind, schools and the means of learning shall forever be encouraged." The sequence is significant: "religion" before morality, and that before knowledge.

One basic purpose of the public schools, then, according to the First Congress, was to foster "religion," which clearly meant, at that time, the teaching of Christian ethics. At that time in history this was the common, if not the universal, definition of the term religion.[5]

Religion based on the Christian ethic was far more integrated into the actual public school curriculum than these historical facts might suggest. Textbooks referred to God without embarrassment, and public schools considered one of their major tasks to be the development of character through the teaching of Christian ethics.

The influence of William Holmes McGuffey, a Presbyterian educator and philosopher, was remarkable. His *Eclectic Readers* were published in 1836, and from that year until 1920—two years after Mississippi became the last state to institute a public school system—his books sold more than 120 million copies, a total that put them in a class with only the Bible and *Webster's Dictionary.*[6]

Historian Henry Steele Commager, in an introduction for a reissue of *McGuffey's Fifth Reader,* writes:

> What was the nature of the morality that permeated the *Readers?* It was deeply religious, and . . . religion then meant a Protestant Christianity. . . . The world of the *McGuffeys* was a world where no one questioned the truths of the Bible or their relevance to everyday contact. . . . The *Readers,* therefore, are filled with stories from the Bible, and tributes to its truth and beauty.

Thus, McGuffey's *Readers* stressed, as did the Northwest Ordinance, "religion, morality, and knowledge" in that order.

The fact that the Christian ethical system permeated the early American culture is important from the standpoint that such an influence was favorable to Christian education and the family. The conflicts that so often exist between the school and the home and between the state and the church today were, by and large, not present in nineteenth-century America.

The common stand of the Christian ethic gave both school and home a compatible base. With the absence of the compatibility factor, we have seen the decline of both the family and the integrity of education.

The State Schools

The diversity that characterized early education eventually gave way to the monolithic state educational system we have today. The process began in the mid-nineteenth century.

Horace Mann and his philosophy were a key turning point in education in America. Mann was a faithful Unitarian and a religious man. Mann's philosophy is summed up in a 1972 biography:

> What the church had been for medieval man, the public school must now become for democratic and rational man. God would be

replaced by the concept of the Public Good, sin and guilt by the more positive virtues of Victorian morality . . .[7]

Education is not only perceived to be religious or "messianic" in character, but as this statement indicates, it is also collectivist in nature.[8]

Moreover, the new state educational system would produce a new type of citizen:

> All of this was now possible if only reasonable men and women would join together to create a well-managed system of schooling, where educators could manipulate and control learning as effectively as the confident new breed of engineers managed the industrial processes at work in their burgeoning textile factories and iron and steel mills. For the first time in the history of western man, it seemed possible for an intellectual and moral elite to effect mass behavioral changes and bring about a new golden age of enlightened ethics, humanism, and affluence.[9]

This new breed of men and women, therefore, were to be behaviorally controlled products of the state system.

We have already discussed John Dewey and his predominant influence in modern state education. His views, in large part, still form the foundation of state education in this country.

In particular, Dewey expresssed a dislike for Christianity. In his legendary work *A Common Faith* (1934) Dewey said: "I cannot understand how any realization of the democratic ideal as a vital moral and spiritual ideal in human affairs is possible without surrender of the conception of the basic division to which supernatural Christianity is committed."[10]

The doctrine to which Dewey was referring is that of the division of mankind into the saved and the unsaved. It clearly created an insurmountable roadblock to Dewey's concept of "progressive education." Thus, it became essential for Christian theism and all the moral absolutes it embraces to be systematically removed from public education.

Dewey saw education as an instrument to control society. In his "Pedagogic Creed" Dewey wrote:

> I believe that
> —education is the fundamental method of social progress and reform.

—every teacher should realize the dignity of his calling; that he is a social servant set apart for the maintenance of proper social order and the securing of the right social growth.

—in this way the teacher is always the prophet of the true God and the usherer in of the true kingdom of God.[11]

The "true God" to which Dewey refers is collective man or humanity.

In the name of "humanity" and "human rights," the public schools have, since Dewey, been secularized. The great questions of God, freedom, immortality, and moral behavior towards fellow-men once addressed by the public schools are hardly touched now. In fact, much of this is *by force of law* forbidden.

The heads of the young, as University of Chicago professor Allan Bloom notes, are stuffed with jargon derived from the despair of European thinkers, repackaged for American consumption, and presented as the foundation for a pluralistic society.[12] As Bloom writes:

That jargon becomes a substitute for real experiences and instinct; one suspects that modern thought has produced an artificial soul to replace the old one supplied by nature, which was full of dangerous longings, loves, hates, and cures. The new soul's language consists of terms like *value, ideology, self, commitment, identity*— every word derived from recent German philosophy, and each carrying a heavy baggage of dubious theoretical interpretation of which its users are blissfully unaware.[13]

The new soul, a secular one, was the ultimate goal of those who formed the presuppositional base of public education. Their wishes have been fulfilled. The football being tossed about in the education game, so to speak, is the child. Our future generations are at stake.

Unfortunately, the presuppositional base undergirding modern American education is in some aspects what Adolf Hitler had in mind when he considered the end of education. For instance, in 1937 Hitler declared that the "new Reich will give its youth to no one, but will itself take youth and give to youth its own education and its own upbringing."[14]

The public education system in this country is obviously not yet on the same level as that of Nazi Germany. The same philosophical presuppositions, however, essentially undergird both systems.

Another Brick in the Wall

With the rise of modern statism, the family has ceased to be a safety zone of freedom because many of the basic functions of the family have been subsumed by the modern state. The state has claimed vast areas which properly belong to the family.

Nowhere is this more evident than in the public education system where the state has proved to be an incompetent substitute for the family, with devastating consequences for society as a whole. This fact is tellingly stated in a 1976 *New York Times* article:

> As American children return to school, many conscientious parents are genuinely uncertain whether they may be delivering their children into enemy territory. . . . Much of America's popular culture adds up to a conspiracy to destroy the innocence of youth and to force upon children premature knowledge and ways of acting that they can understand intellectually but not cope with emotionally. . . . The new sophistication . . . is more than a passing phenomenon of the 60's . . . its evil effects can be seen today in the grim statistics on suicide, now the second leading cause of death among persons aged 12 to 24 and occurring at a rate twice what it was a decade ago, and the soaring venereal disease rates. . . . The distinctive theme of this new sophistication is the absence of restraint, but good families frame their children's lives with love . . . and with restrictions. These restraints are not idle do's and don'ts. They represent accumulated folk wisdom at the child's self preservation, at protecting him against dangers he cannot fully recognize or foresee.[15]

The public education system is an indispensable part of the modern state. Yet, public education, both academically and morally, has been a failure.

Statist education in the United States has led to one of the highest illiteracy rates in our history. As a 1980 *Time* magazine article indicates: "A Government . . . survey . . . reports that . . . the achievement of U.S. 17-year-olds has dropped regularly over the decade."[16]

Newsweek magazine reported a year later:

Academic standards seem to get flimsier by the year. Costs per pupil are rising at the same time enrollments are falling and budgets shrinking. Administrators are overwhelmed with paperwork; teachers have to contend with drugs and alcohol, truancy and vandalism, apathy, and ignorance. Some have plainly given up, victims of a classroom epidemic called teacher burnout. Others are plainly incompetent, unable to cope with their problem students or teach their normal ones. Schools sometimes seem more like detention halls than groves of academe. Backtalk is routine and felonious assault is more common than anyone wants to admit.[17]

Modern public education has unwittingly given this country a generation of torn youth. Some interesting parallels exist between pre-Hitler youth of Germany and today's American youth.

The German youth of the late 1920s and 1930s had become alienated from the older generation. They were questioning the old order. Pessimism had permeated a country that had recently suffered a humiliating defeat in World War I.

The traditional authorities of school, church, and family had become suspect in Germany. As H. W. Koch, a former Hitler Youth member himself, writes:

They left home at weekends and during school or university holidays with tent, rucksack, and guitar, hiking through Germany north to south, east to west, discovering for themselves the quiet beauty of the German countryside . . . in search of something new. They turned to an age gone by, epitomized by the romantic element in most of Wagner's operas, and around the campfires they sat singing the ballads of old. Folklore experienced a renaissance.[18]

It was from this anarchic state that Hitler built his Hitler Youth Movement. From fewer than one million in 1932, Hitler's Youth had swollen to over eight million in 1939, all dedicated to serving the Führer.

American youth find themselves in a similar situation as that faced by the German youth of the 1930s. Allan Bloom writes, "In feeling as well as in speech, a large segment of our young are open, open to every 'lifestyle.' But the fatal consequence of this openness has been the withering of their belief in their own way of life and their capacity to generate goals."[19]

American youth have little direction in a culture that, through its educational system, teaches a "do your own thing" mentality. The frustration from our youth's directionlessness has fostered a nihilistic pessimism.

Our present age may be best reflected in and through the rock group Pink Floyd. In the movie *The Wall* the group sings:

> We don't need no education
> We don't need no thought control
> No dark sarcasm in the classroom
> Teacher, leave them kids alone
> Hey, teacher, leave them kids alone.
>
> All in all, it's just another brick in the wall
> All in all, you're just another brick in the wall.[20]

The Christian Schools

Hitler understood very well the power of state-controlled public education. In a 1933 speech he remarked:

> When an opponent declares, "I will not come over to your side," I calmly say, "Your child belongs to us already. . . . What are you? You will pass on. Your descendants, however, now stand in the new camp. In a short time they will know nothing else but this new community."[21]

Some German parents did not want their children indoctrinated by the Nazi state and sought to keep their children from joining the Hitler Youth Movement. These parents eventually were met with heavy prison sentences.

If the parents refused to surrender their children, the next step was legal coercion. William Shirer has written: "Recalcitrant parents were warned that their children would be taken away from them and put into orphanages or other homes unless they enrolled."[22]

Hitler did not stop with the children and parents. In 1936 *he abolished all Christian schools* in Germany. Two years later all public school teachers were ordered to resign from any denominational organization.[23]

Shades of this type of coercion have already surfaced in the United States. The same legal pressure and imprisonment is used to force parents of Christian school students and administrators of Christian schools to accept state regulation of the schools. Moreover, there are now instances of abduction of children by the state to orphanages and other state facilities.

One of the best-known cases concerns the 1981 padlocking of the church doors of Faith Baptist Church in Louisville, Nebraska. The crime? The church operated an unlicensed Christian school. The pastor was later jailed for continuing the operation of the school.

With attempts by the state to control Christian schools, the issue is made more complex because most of the Christian schools are operated as ministries of local churches. Thus, the constitutional doctrine of the separation of church and state comes into play.

In the Faith Baptist Church case, the State of Nebraska successfully argued through the courts that it has such a great responsibility to see that its citizens are properly equipped through education to function in society that it must impose requirements on Christian schools. To that end the state sought to license the school, certify the teachers, and approve the curriculum of the church school.

This amounts to an attempt to control the content of what the children in Christian schools receive. The state education agencies have generally failed to respect the wishes of religious parents who send their children to Christian schools. Many parents send their children to such schools so they will not receive the content normally taught in the public schools.

The church involved asserted that licensure and other state controls violated its religious doctrines. Such controls, argued the church, require the church to submit to unbiblical requirements.

The State of Nebraska argued that curriculum approval, licensing, and teacher certification are only "minimal intrusions" upon the religious practice of church schools. However, the United States Supreme Court has consistently held that even minimal intrusions on religious practice must be justified by what it calls a "compelling state interest." In other words, the state must show an interest of such a great magnitude to justify not allowing an exemption for those whose religion the state regulation infringes.

In the case of a church school, the state's compelling interest, if any, is that the children are receiving a quality education or, at least, a comparable education to those children who attend the public schools.

In the great majority of cases that have gone to trial over church schools, the quality of education has never really been in doubt. *In fact, in most instances children attending Christian schools score higher on the standard tests than do those students who attend public schools.*[24]

In the Faith Baptist Church case no evidence was presented at the trial by the state that the school was failing to provide a quality education. As Professor James Carper has noted:

> If children in unapproved religious schools perform as well or better than their public school counterparts, and some data suggest this is the case, a legitimate question can be raised concerning the validity of not only curriculum and teacher certification requirements, but the whole regulatory and licensing process as well.[25]

The Supreme Court of Nebraska, in a poorly reasoned decision, upheld the closing of the church because the school had failed to comply with the state's regulatory scheme.[26] The United States Supreme Court later refused to hear the case because, it said, there was "no substantial federal question" involved.

This case merely represents the tip of the iceberg. In some Christian school cases parents have been arrested and prosecuted for failing to send their children to state "approved" schools. This will increase in light of the recent surge of home school programs where parents have routinely been cited for truancy for that offense. Several years ago there were at least 10,000 families educating their children at home. In 1982 the figure was estimated at one million.[27]

The main obstacle to home education programs are compulsory education laws. Often these laws compel state-certified teachers and licensure.

Many courts have upheld these requirements. For example, in 1981 and 1982 the West Virginia and Virginia Supreme Courts, respectively, ruled against home school parents. This is all in light of the fact that licensure and teacher certification have not (and possibly cannot) be proved either to maintain or to improve education quality.

We can expect parents to continue challenging state education laws. This will result in further state prosecution of parents. There is a colossal irony here. The same state that sees no reason to prevent a minor from having an abortion (or to require telling her parents about it) will prosecute parents who care enough for their children to seek an alternative to the public school system by providing them with home education.

Four strong arguments can be made in support of parental control of their children's education and Christian schools. First, the state, if religious freedom is to have any meaning, should accommodate the religious beliefs of the parents. Second, the constitutional protection of parental choice among educational alternatives only has meaning if private schools can offer an educational experience truly distinct from that offered in the public schools. Third, parents who send their children to Christian schools care a great deal about their children's educational experience and are also actively involved in that experience. Fourth, the Christian school and home school choice is a family issue. "Families," Alvin Toffler writes, "should be encouraged to take a larger—not smaller—role in the education of the young. Parents willing to teach their children at home should be aided by the schools, not regarded as freaks or lawbreakers. And parents should have more, not less, influence on the schools."28

The state has not heeded this and similar well-founded advice. Instead, the state has often asserted its power and control over schools and parents for no other reason than that the school programs are not state-approved. Unfortunately, this has been at the expense of the children on whose behalf the state is purportedly acting.

A Funeral Service?

Whatever philosophy controls the educational system will eventually play a large part in controlling the way people think and act. What we see happening in our country today is to a large extent the result of people acting out what they learned in school.

Man with the secular soul is now with us. This is a good sign to some.

Paul Blanshard, an author and leading humanist thinker, gives us an indication of such thinking in *The Humanist,* the official journal of the American Humanist Association. In an article entitled "Three Cheers for Our Secular State" he writes: "Our seventy-five years in this century, all of which I have lived and relished, have been a good seventy-five years, full of rebellion against religious superstition, inspired by developing science, and increasingly open to religious realism. I doubt that any span in human history has carried the world farther along the road to honest doubt."

Blanshard states that his "hero" in this movement is the United States Supreme Court because of its decisions removing various religious practices from the classroom. He then tells us why America has moved so far down the path of secularism:

> I think that the most important factor moving us toward a secular society has been the educational factor. Our schools may not teach Johnny to read properly, but the fact that Johnny is in school until he is sixteen tends to lead toward the elimination of religious superstition. The average American child now acquires a high-school education, and this militates against Adam and Eve and all other myths of alleged history. . . . When I was one of the editors of *The Nation* in the twenties, I wrote an editorial explaining that golf and intelligence were the two primary reasons that men did not attend church. Perhaps I would now say golf and a high-school diploma.[29]

Basically what Paul Blanshard is saying is that public education is repsonsible for what he hopes will be the total destruction of Christian theism. In fact, he seems to imply that such a goal should be the purpose of education.

Similar thinking can be seen in the writings of G. Richard Bozarth. In *The American Atheist* he says: "We Atheists today . . . must admit that for corpses . . . Old Yahweh and his sidekick JC Superstar are taking a long time to stop twitching and grow old."

In speaking of ways in which to kill God, Bozarth says:

> And how does a god die? Quite simply because all his religionists have been converted to another religion, and there is no one left to make children believe they need him. . . . We need only insure that our schools teach only secular knowledge. . . . If we could achieve this god would indeed be shortly due for a funeral service.[30]

John J. Dunphy, again writing in a 1983 issue of *The Humanist,* proclaims:

> I am convinced that *the battle for humankind's future must be waged and won in the public school classroom* by teachers who correctly perceive their role as the proselytizers of a new faith: a religion of humanity that recognizes and respects the spark of what theologians call divinity in every human being. These teachers must embody the same selfless dedication as the most rabid fundamentalist preachers, for they will be ministers of another sort, utilizing a classroom instead of a pulpit to convey humanist values in whatever subject they teach, regardless of the educational level—preschool day care or large state university. *The classroom must and will become an arena of conflict between the old and the new—the rotting corpse of Christianity, together with all its adjacent evils and misery, and the new faith of humanism, resplendent in its promise of a world in which the never-realized Christian ideal of "love thy neighbor" will finally be achieved.*[31]

The thesis of these men, in reflecting John Dewey, is simple: if a child in the public school spends the greater amount of his time in a secular setting, it will have the effect of purging the child of what he or she may be taught in the family or at church concerning theistic religion. In practical terms, this has occurred.

However, in its wake the public education system has declined. Its secularization has brought about the private school movement, which has given us some greatly needed diversity. The private school movement (Protestant, Catholic, Jewish or otherwise) will, it is hoped, continue to grow and remain free of government control.

By the same token, a hole must be forged in the secularization process of public schools to allow for freedom of speech of religious persons. If not, then freedom for all public arenas may be threatened.

Logically, if free speech is not allowed in one public place (such as a public school), then sooner or later it will be prohibited on the public street corner. Although this would not signal a funeral service for God, it would certainly mean the end of true freedom. And the state would become fully what it is now partially—the slavemaster of free souls.

9 SUBDUING THE CHURCH

The secular state will invitably lead to authoritarian government in one form or another. Such a state has no absolute reference point. It is bound by no philosophy except one of its own making; it recognizes no right as absolute and no Creator as the father of rights, morality, or human dignity. With a relativistic philosophy, the secular state can do or declare anything and justify it on the basis that it is for the good of the people.

The individual in such a society is at the mercy of the elite who control the state. Abortion or euthanasia can be characterized as beneficial on such shallow grounds as population control or the "rights" of pregnant women.

The secular state will operate without any restraint. It will not operate under the law. It is under no law except its own which can be altered arbitrarily to meet the situation.

In the past the illegitimate state, whether based upon majority rule or complete dictatorial rule by one man or an elite, has claimed to be the absolute. This means that the state possesses total jurisdiction and power over the people.

Moreover, such a state will claim it is under no one. The state is the great umbrella under which all things must fit, even the Creator or conceptions of him.

Therefore, as we often hear today, it will claim to be secular and indifferent or neutral to religion. This claim is, of course, a fictitious one since neutrality toward religion is nonexistent.

The Secular State
Stated desire to have a purely secular state, it must be emphasized, is of relatively recent origin. In fact, throughout

most of history the state has been the religious order of man and the central vehicle of his religious life.

We are accustomed to thinking of the church as the religious institution and the state as simply the political ordering of man's life. This is erroneous thinking. For example, the ruler's office was considered holy both in Greece and Rome.

It wasn't until the French Revolution in 1789 that the concept of a deliberately secular state emerged as a full-fledged entity. There, however, "reason" was enthroned as the goddess of the state. Even in its secular form, the state is religious.

The word "secular" comes from the Latin *saecularis,* meaning "a race, generation, age, the times of the world." Its basic meaning is this: the secular is the worldly or temporal as against the spiritual or eternal.

The secular is that which belongs to the state as distinguished from the religious or the church. The secular is concerned with the world rather than with Heaven.

The secular state, then, is that state which denies any transcendental claim upon itself. Nothing is above or over such a state (including God).

Although the secular state may deny the existence of the eternal, it will often act as if the eternal exists. Such a state will crown its monarch or install its premiere or president with religious ceremony.

Under the concept of the secular state, there is no appeal except to the state and its officials. There can be no appeal to the Creator as we have in the Declaration of Independence. The Creator becomes either subject to the whims of the state or he is irrelevant to the basic needs of man.

This is precisely the statement of the United States Supreme Court decisions which ruled mandatory prayer, Bible reading, and the posting of the Ten Commandments illegal in the public schools of America: God is irrelevant. Thus, a state is secular if it is hostile toward theistic religion—either by overt *opposition* as in the Soviet Union or by less overt *discrimination* vis-a-vis other institutions as in America.

Permission to Exist

The modern secular state, as in ancient Rome, defines what

is and is not permitted in terms of religion. Tertullian (160-240) opposed this fact during the times of the Roman Empire.

No god became a god until approved by the Roman senate, which officially promoted heroes to that status. Unless the gods gave satisfaction to men, there would be no deification for them; that is, the god would first have to appease man. These men (or heroes) became gods, of course, simply because they expressed the "genius" of the city of Rome. They supposedly manifested the inherent divinity of the state.

In this country the federal government, through such agencies as the Internal Revenue Service, is moving perilously close to defining what is and is not permitted in terms of religion (much like that of the Roman Empire). Although the Internal Revenue Code contains no definition of a church (because it would be unconstitutional under the First Amendment), the I.R.S. has made reference to the following list of characteristics in determining the tax-exempt status of an organization "claiming" to be a church:

1. A distinct legal existence
2. A recognized creed and form of worship
3. A definite and distinct ecclesiastical government
4. A formal code of doctrine and discipline
5. A distinct religious history
6. A membership not associated with any church or denomination
7. A complete organization of ordained ministers ministering to their congregations
8. Ordained ministers selected after completing prescribed courses of study
9. A literature of its own
10. Established places of worship
11. Regular congregations
12. Regular religious services
13. Sunday schools for the religious instruction of the young
14. Schools for the preparation of its ministers.

Although the I.R.S. does not require all fourteen points to be met, it does use this as the standard.

The early church, according to I.R.S. rules, may very well have *not* been considered a "legal" entity. Moreover, the fact that the I.R.S. has conducted sweeping audits of churches (which have been generally upheld by the courts) and applied the tax codes to churches is a clear indication that we may be on our way to state-mandated religious guidelines. This may be true even though such guidelines have not been made the official public regulations of the I.R.S.

Some claim that the very status granted to the church as a tax-exempt organization is "insulting."[1] A church is classified, when exempted, as a section 501(c) (3) operation under the Internal Revenue Code. This is a classification for a wide variety of charitable trusts. It can include a humane society, a pet cemetery, a lodge, or a local charity, besides religious and other organizations.

The federal government is increasingly claiming the right to govern all these section 501(c) (3) organizations as public trusts that are required to conform to public policy (that is, whatever the federal government deems right at a particular time) and to use all funds, assets, and properties for the general public. The implication is that the church is permitted to exist only because it benefits the public, rather than because of its own right to exist as God's institution, and that it should be under the authority of the state, rather than autonomous.

The Beginnings

As we have seen, secularism is a closed system. As such, it will eventually seek to eliminate alternative viewpoints.

The secular state wants no competition in the arena of ideas. It is ideas that totalitarian states fear most. That is why, although such states will suffer the church to exist, they will allow no dissemination of Christian ideas, particularly to children because they represent the future. Thus, evangelization is outlawed, and parental instruction of children in religious belief is forbidden.

Logically, then, the secular state will work to control and circumscribe the church. If this proves impossible it will somehow persecute the church.

Historian Erik von Kuehnelt-Leddihn writes that as humanism begins to dominate the state the consequence is "complete hostile annexation of the church ('Josephinistic' establishments under state control) or persecution by separation. Religion is then removed from the marketplace and the school, later from other domains of public life. The state will not tolerate any gods besides itself."[2]

Historically there have been two major stages in the attack on the church. First, the state and its agencies are secularized. Second, the state attacks every prerogative or privilege of the church in an indirect manner so that, in disguised fashion, its right to exist is denied.

In the name of freedom, the Supreme Court has, in large measure, accomplished the secularization of the state. And as the state has been secularized, the prerogatives of the church have come under attack. For example, the Internal Revenue Service's claim that it can assume authority over churches and revoke their tax exemption is a way of placing the church under the dominance of the state.

Another area in which the church is presently denied its prerogatives is by way of zoning laws. Zoning laws radiate an aura of progress and civic improvement. They also have a basic appeal to the desire of people to improve their property (while steadily infringing on their property rights). Through zoning laws countless churches and church schools have been denied building permits and, thereby, the right to exist in a general area.

The secularistic state recognizes, however, that Christianity cannot be completely eradicated. Therefore, the state attempts to restrict the freedom of the church in a number of ways.

Underground evangelist Jan Pit in *Persecution: It Will Never Happen Here?* writes that in Iron Curtain countries the following restrictions in religious freedom are prevalent:

1. The churches and their members must be registered. This becomes a means for the state to control church functions and to have access to the membership rolls.
2. Christians are permitted to worship and to talk about the Lord only inside the registered church building. Public evangelism is prohibited in most Communist countries.
3. Christians are forbidden to teach religion to children; therefore Sunday schools and youth gatherings are not allowed. Even within the home, Christian training is not to take place.

4. Christians are given the less desirable menial jobs: their children are not allowed a university education. They are, in effect, second class citizens.[3]

Jan Pit's analysis here is intriguing when one realizes that all of the four restrictions have, in some form, been instituted in this country. For example, in the United States tax laws require a form of registration for exemption purposes. All employers, including churches, are required to possess federal tax numbers. Moreover, there are cases and laws that require Christian schools (most of them church schools) and institutions to be licensed and regulated by the state. Also, Christian schools that are church ministries are not allowed a tax exemption unless they file and receive approval of a formal application with the federal government (although currently churches are exempt without filing such an application).

There are also cases and laws which hold that worship services cannot be held in private homes, usually under zoning laws and regulations. And we all know that prayer and Bible reading are unconstitutional in the public schools in America. Will there come a time when Christians will not be able to find significant employment or attain a sufficient education?

The Soviet Example
Ultimately the secular state seeks to restrict church activities to the sanctuary. This is for control purposes. When it has accomplished this, the state then regulates worship. This is readily apparent in the Soviet Union. And it is carried forth in the name of religious freedom.

An example is the Soviet Constitution which provides:

Article 52. Freedom of conscience, that is the right to profess any religion or not to profess any religion, to perform religious rites or to conduct atheist propaganda shall be guaranteed for all citizens of the USSR. . . . The church in the USSR shall be separated from the state and the school from the church.

Notice that not only is separation of church and state provided for but also separation of church and school. The Soviets know quite well that if the state can control education and indoctrinate children in atheism, then, no matter what is taught in the sanctuary, it will be scoffed at.

John A. Armstrong in *Ideology, Politics, and Government in the Soviet Union* (1974) illustrates that the Soviet practice contradicts its Constitution:

> Severe sentences have been imposed for organizing Sunday schools. Legally, religious parents may instruct their children at home. Despite its reaffirmation by jurists, even this freedom is dubious. The 1968 Principles of Marriage and Family Law provide that a court may remove a child from parents "if the child is endangered by remaining." Still earlier, a father was convicted for "forcing" religion on his daughter, and the children of religious parents were removed to the custody of a brother who had renounced religion.[4]

Subduing the Church

One method used by the government in recent years in bringing the church under its control is the auditing power of the I.R.S. There are general reasons why many churches have resisted the audits.

First, the audits generally give the government the power to go through virtually all the records of the church. Thus, the government learns even the most intimate details about the operation of certain churches, without any real justification but with much danger of governmental mischief.

Second, audits are conducted on a particular church when the purpose is to determine if that church is a church within the eyes of I.R.S. officials. Traditionally, it has never been the province of the state in this country to determine what is and is not a church.

The attempts by the I.R.S. at asserting its authority over the church have resulted in some horrible court cases. For example, a pastor of an independent Bible church in Texas was jailed in February 1980 by a federal district judge. The offense? The pastor refused to surrender church records to the I.R.S. The I.R.S. had demanded that the church surrender all its records and the names and addresses of church members and contributors for an administrative examination. The church was also required to complete an extensive questionnaire.

On appeal, a United States Court of Appeals ruled partially in favor of the church. The court, however, in denying the I.R.S. the authority to issue a blanket summons for information from the church, held that the church, in order to retain its tax-exempt status, "must allow the government access to information."

In another case with very similar facts, an I.R.S. summons seeking to require the pastor of a church to produce church records was held by a different United States Circuit Court of Appeals to be within constitutional parameters and, therefore, not an infringement of the First Amendment.

To illustrate how pervasive the problem has become, the situation in which the Church of Christian Liberty of Brookfield, Wisconsin, has found itself deserves a close look. The I.R.S. contacted this small independent church, demanding the records of the church's day school to confirm that the school was operating a nondiscriminatory policy. The church refused on biblical and constitutional grounds, but invited the I.R.S. to visit the church and school.

Shortly thereafter, two I.R.S. agents did visit the church school and sat through a chapel service as well as observed classes and the multiracial makeup of the small student body. At the end of the visit, the agents demanded to see the financial records of the school which are, in fact, church records. Again the church refused.

The pastor went so far as to travel to the local I.R.S. offices to explain his biblical and constitutional reasons (based upon the separation of church and state) for not giving over the church records to the federal government.

Several months later an I.R.S. summons was served on the church which demanded all its records. Among other things, the summons asked for the following church records:

1. All financial records
2. All documents related to organizational structure (such as Articles of Incorporation, bylaws, etc.)
3. All correspondence files
4. All records of the names and addresses of persons who served as officers or ministers of the church
5. All minutes of any meetings held by the church

6. One sample of each brochure, pamphlet, handout, program, or other literature pertaining to the church's ministry
7. All records reflecting the names of any employees, associates, or ministers of the church and particularly any reflecting the names of individuals who had been presented credentials of ministry (ordination, etc.)
8. All documents reflecting any sacerdotal functions performed by the church (marriages, baptisms, etc.)
9. All documents reflecting the principles, creeds, precepts, doctrines, practices, and disciplines espoused by the church, and,
10. All documents reflecting membership requirements of the church.

After receiving the summons, the pastor of the church again traveled to the regional I.R.S. office in Milwaukee to explain why the church could not give the federal government complete and total access to the church records, a privilege not even members of the church enjoy. The pastor informed the agents that he had nothing to hide and that if they so desired there were certain items on the list that the I.R.S. could see in order to establish this church as a legitimate church.

Shortly thereafter, an agent from the I.R.S. visited the church and was shown, under constitutional protest, the articles of incorporation of the church which indicated that the church had enjoyed tax-exempt status with the I.R.S. for some ten years. Among other items, the agent was also shown documentation reflecting that the pastor had performed marriages and baptisms; Sunday worship bulletins; the constitution of the church; and the Westminster Confession of Faith. The agent also spoke with board members as well as members of the church.

This information, however, was not sufficient to assure the agent that this indeed was a legitimate church. The agent indicated that he needed all the records of the church. The church again refused.

Next, the I.R.S. took the church to court in seeking enforcement of its summons. Both a federal magistrate and a federal district court judge found in favor of the church in holding that the summons was overbroad in asking for too much information.

All the information demanded, it was held, was not necessary to determine whether or not the church was legitimate.

Unfortunately, the I.R.S. did not stop there. It appealed the case to the United States Court of Appeals, which overturned the lower courts. The court of appeals in a sweeping decision held that the I.R.S. had, in effect, total authority to conduct inclusive audits of churches.

This case was immediately appealed to the United States Supreme Court which, in the spring of 1982, refused to hear the church's plea for help.

The Curse

Many churches, when contacted by the I.R.S., have submitted to the state's authority and have allowed the state to conduct a search for information. The church, once considered sacred, is now in the eyes of many state officials no different than any other entity.

Should the church, however, prostrate itself before the state?

The Bible in rather simple fashion declares that we are to render unto Caesar the things that are Caesar's. But does the church belong to Caesar? In Ephesians 1:22 we are instructed that the church is Christ's.

Moreover, does the church need approval of the government to function? Has not Christ, by establishing individual churches, already approved of their existence?

The Apostle Paul admonishes Christians in 1 Corinthians 6 not to take their church disagreements into the secular courts. It is not a biblical function of the government to judge church matters. It is a function of the church itself under the leading of the Holy Spirit, and ultimately Christ, to establish how it will conduct its activities. Certainly it is no business of the state to determine such things.

In addition, opening the gates of the church to government bureaucrats may find us in the same dilemma as Hezekiah in 2 Kings 20. Hezekiah opened the doors of his kingdom to the King of Babylon, and "there was nothing in his house, nor in all his dominion, that Hezekiah shewed them not" (v. 13). For this, a strong curse was pronounced on Hezekiah (vv. 14-18).

The trappings of freedom yet remain in this country. While there is time, we should resist the state's illegitimate claims over the church. If not, like Hezekiah, we may find ourselves under a curse from which there is no escape.

10 PRIORITIES AND RESISTANCE

Shortly after his exile from the Soviet Union, Aleksandr Solzhenitsyn asked:

> Are we prepared to learn from the past? Are people living in freedom able to learn from those living in need? Can the lesson they have learned be taught to a free world? Yes, it can, but who wants to learn? Our proud skyscrapers point heavenward and they say: It will never happen here. But *it will happen.* The revolution will come. Tragically, however, the free West will only believe it when it is no longer free. To quote a Russian proverb, "When it happens you will know it is true, but then it is too late."[1]

No Concessions, No Excuses

Solzhenitsyn posed a key question: "Are we prepared to learn from the past?"

Recent Christian activism is a good sign. It means that some have learned from the past. It also means that Christians are now reacting to present crises. The staying power of the new activism, however, remains to be seen.

The stranglehold that false pietism yet exerts over Christendom is a troubling sign. This view stresses only the personal "salvation" experience. Bible study becomes simplistic, and any form of intellectualism is considered unspiritual.

False pietism, as it gained predominance in the early twentieth century, adopted a religious form of Platonism (the belief that the spiritual world is somehow superior to and above the physical-temporal world). It created an unbiblical dichotomy between the spiritual and temporal worlds. Christians, as a consequence, eventually withdrew their influence from politics, education, and other vital areas of life. Christianity then became privatized, and its effect on the real world which exists outside the church was lessened.

The fact that evangelization is to be the preeminent concern of the church is not questioned here. However, modern Christians have, as a whole, been poor evangelists because they do not understand the true nature of evangelism.

Evangelism is more than leading people to Christ. That is the first step.

The church must also prepare individual Christians to redeem their culture—that is, to be salt (Matthew 5:13). Unfortunately the Christian leadership has done little to externalize the gospel and make its application relevant to our times.

As a consequence, Christians have fallen into the abyss of secularism. "[T]he Christian mind," writes Harry Blamires, "has succumbed to the secular drift with a degree of weakness and nervelessness unmatched in Christian history. It is difficult to do justice in words to the complete loss of intellectual morale in the twentieth-century Church. . . . There is no longer a Christian mind."[2]

Recent increases in church membership are pointed to as a hopeful sign. Pollster George Gallup, however, sees worrisome trends that "threaten to undermine the efforts of churches and to stall the religious momentum." Chief among these troublesome trends is "the glaring lack of knowledge of the Ten Commandments, the nation's religious heritage, and the central tenets of religion" by those calling themselves Christians.[3] As *Newsweek* reports:

> Despite the fact that the majority of Americans say they accept the Bible as the word of God, a comprehensive 1979 Gallup survey found that only 49 percent of Protestants and 44 percent of Roman Catholics could name as many as four of the Ten Commandments and less than half of the respondents said they turn first to the Scriptures for guidance in times of crisis.[4]

We are, therefore, presented with a major ethical crisis in this country. William Barclay writes:

> [T]he crisis of the present is not theological; it is ethical. Christian theology is not really under attack, for there are few outside the

Church sufficiently interested in it to assail it, and the internecine wars of the technical theologians are not of any great interest to the general public.[5]

Sad to say, the Bible is simply no longer the norm it used to be. If anything, our modern culture is predisposed against the Christian ethic. This means that "[t]here has never been a time when the discussion of the Christian Ethic has been more necessary and more relevant."[6]

Christians have a massive educational task facing them. Education in contemporary society, however, must come in many forms: writing, speaking, protesting, picketing, defending, and even suing in court, in addition to other forms of making issues public.

Christians should not be afraid to challenge the modern secularistic culture. The present "air raid shelter" mentality of Christians will not alter the course of society. Timidity, likewise, will not bring about change. C. S. Lewis said:

> As Christians we are tempted to make unnecessary concessions to those outside the Faith. We give in too much. . . . We must show our Christian colours if we are to be true to Jesus Christ. We cannot remain silent and concede everything away.[7]

Concession and dismay mark modern Christendom. Like ten of the twelve spies sent out by Moses to report on the military capacities of the Canaanite cultures, our reports are filled with dismay. Yet Rahab was to tell the spies of the next generation that "as soon as we heard these things, our hearts did melt, neither did their remain any more courage in any man, because of you: for the Lord your God, he is God in heaven above, and in earth beneath" (Joshua 2:11).

Therefore, the battle cry of faithful Christians should be that Christ is Lord of all things in Heaven and earth. He is not simply Lord of Heaven above and impotent on the earth. He is Lord of the entire cosmos.

The misinterpretation of Christ's words—that his kingdom is not of this world (John 18:36)—should be finally given the burial it deserves. In this verse Christ was asserting to Pilate that his source of authority, of human sovereignty, of Lordship was not an earthly source, but heavenly. It has nothing to do with Christ's authority over all things.

The newspapers, the entertainment media, and the universities likewise can speak of little else but defeat and alienation. The secularists see their world crumbling about them. What an opportunity to speak a consistent Christian message into the secularist vacuum. Modern Christians, however, often fill their sermons, evangelistic crusades, and bookstores with a false pietism.

Humanists like Anatolia Fraser in *Cromwell: The Lord Protector* have had to remind modern Christians of their own heritage. Why should critiques of modern secularism be left to neoorthodox scholars like Langdon Gilkey who, in *Maker of Heaven and Earth,* has written one of the better books available on the implications of the doctrine of creation—something Gilkey does not even believe in its historic form?

Christians naively believe that they can *retreat* (note that Christian seminars are often called retreats) into a zone of social and political impotence and, therefore, social and political irresponsibility (just as they have done for over a century). However, with the acids of relativism eroding the foundations of humanism, the social buffers are disappearing.

Drugs, pornography, lawlessness, economic disruption, witchcraft, random murders, abortion, terrorism, and all the rest of secularism's children no longer respect the doors of the churches the way they used to. Like Joab, contemporary Christians are discovering that the horns of the altar no longer protect them from destruction (1 Kings 2:28, 34). They can no longer be "nice" Christians, the beneficiaries of the endless fruits of a former Christian culture, hiding in their "nice" colleges, "nice" churches, and "nice" ministries.

As a whole, modern evangelism, because of its pietistic base, has had little effect on our modern culture. As a consequence, the enemy is at the gates. Coupled with the fact that humanism is at the end of the road spiritually, nothing is left to hold society together except brute force.

There are no safety zones in the combat of faith. The only way to be effective is to apply true Christianity consistently to the culture in all its aspects. As underground evangelist Brother Andrew has written:

The first principle for any Christian work is this: the Lord Jesus Christ, who crushed Satan and conquered death, commands us to invade this enemy-occupied world and reclaim it for God. We march under his exclusive authority and are forbidden to make any deals with the foe. No compromises. No concessions. And no excuses![8]

If we are not prepared to do this, then we have not learned the lessons of the past. And we will be bound to repeat them.

Resistance and Strategy

In Matthew 10:16 Christ sets forth the rule for Christians when they find themselves in a hostile climate. They are to be wise. Like the serpent, they must use a calm discretion in fighting for the faith.

This means Christians must be wise in their confrontations with the state. We cannot be caught fighting useless battles that get us nowhere. Time is short and resources are limited. We must use our resources in the way they count the most.

Wisdom dictates, first, that resistance and civil disobedience be carried forth in a biblical manner. Second, wisdom dictates that priorities be established and followed.

Before resorting to civil disobedience, *all* reasonable alternatives should be exhausted. If there is an opportunity to alter the course of events through normal channels (for example, negotiation or legislation) they should be attempted.

Civil disobedience should never be perpetrated for dramatics but for its effectiveness. Throwing goat's blood on the door of an abortion clinic is dramatic. However, it will do little to hinder the performing of abortions.

Resistance and civil disobedience are legitimate reactions to tyrannous acts of the state. Overreaction to such acts, however, can spill over into violence. That we do not want. Unmitigated violence can never be justified.

There is a distinction between force and violence that must be made. Force is a fact of life in our fallen world. Sooner or later every person will use some type of force. As Os Guinness writes:

> Without such a distinction there can be no legitimate justification for authority or discipline of any kind, whether on a parental or on

a presidential level. In a fallen world the ideal of legal justice without the exercise of force is naive. Societies need a police force, a man has the right to defend his wife from assault. A feature of any society which can achieve a measure of freedom within form is that responsibility implies discipline. This is true at the various structural levels of society—in the sphere of the state, business, the community, the school, respectively.[9]

To prevent resistance or civil disobedience from degenerating into taking the law into one's hands, it should be organized and under authority. Vigilantes are not justified under Scripture.

Christians have been drawn off into many minor battles because they lack priorities. If we are to survive the coming years, it will be because Christians and others have focused on the key issues.

The key priority issues are those discussed in this book. In order of their importance they are: the sanctity of human life; the protection of the traditional family, the church and the private school; the freedom of the public arena (including public schools); and the need to assist those who are oppressed for their faith in totalitarian states. This is not a checklist but a list of priorities which must be conscientiously dealt with simultaneously.

Priority One: The Sanctity of Human Life

The sanctity of human life is *the* priority issue. It covers the entire spectrum of threats to human life including abortion, infanticide, and euthanasia. It touches the very nature of man's existence. If not dealt with effectively, it spells the death of this country.

The life issue is the one issue on which all Christians should be able to unite. If Christians cannot unite on this issue, then I seriously doubt there is any issue on which they can unite to bring change.

The Bible speaks strongly to our responsibility toward the spilling of innocent blood. Proverbs 24:11, 12, paraphrased, states:

Rescue those who are unjustly sentenced to death; don't stand back and let them die. Don't try to disclaim responsibility by saying you didn't know about it. For God, who knows all hearts, knows yours, and he knows you knew! And he will reward everyone according to his deeds. *(The Living Bible)*

Historically the church at its best has been quick to associate with the helpless. This is the compassionate heritage of the Christian church. It is the origin of the stories we have of persons who would leave a baby or little child on the steps of a cathedral, knowing that a priest, nun, or clergyman would come and take in that little life and give it love and care.

These examples of compassion were understood as the meaning of true religion. James 1:27 (AV) tells us: "Pure religion and undefiled before God and the Father is this, To visit the fatherless and widows in their affliction, and to keep himself unspotted from the world."

The church should return to its heritage. There is no better place to exhibit this return than in the human life issue. "A child who is left alone, to starve to death, can only be called an orphan. An aborted child is no different; it is an orphan. We have a responsibility, the New Testament tells us, with regard to orphans. A child who is helpless, who is left to die, is, by any definition, an orphan."[10]

If those who say they believe abortion is murder really believe it, *they will do something about it.* Surely if you witnessed your father, mother, brother or sister being carried into a euthanasia clinic on a stretcher you would act, and radically if necessary. The same principle applies to abortion except the child is being carried into the abortion clinic in his or her mother's womb.

Besides legislative efforts and political involvement, both of which are important, Christians can directly affect abortion in other ways. At the least, the number of babies killed can be reduced.

Churches can operate or contribute to pregnancy crisis centers. A telephone hotline can be installed and used to counsel and later to assist pregnant women.

The church should be the first place a pregnant woman comes for help. The church should assist with open homes during and after birth, until the girl is able to get on her feet.

Counselors in the church must be informed about and prepared to deal with the emotional and psychological problems faced by women who are being pressured to have abortions. These women need to know there are alternatives to abortion (such as adoption). They also need to know there is a large body of people standing by, ready to provide life-saving alternatives.

Picketing is another effective way to reduce the number of abortions. Some local churches use their Sunday school buses to pick up and drive their people to abortion clinics to picket.

Counseling women as they enter abortion clinics and also guiding them to a local church-operated pregnancy crisis center have proved to be effective alternatives to abortion. Of course, it is vital to approach an abortion-minded woman in a compassionate and nonderogatory manner in order to be heard and to have any influence.

Picketing accomplishes something other alternatives do not. In a nonviolent, lawful way it brings the issue of abortion to public light. This, coupled with the loss of business, is why abortion clinics abhor and even fight picketing.

Therefore, picketing should not be a symbolic excursion. Instead, it should be a serious attempt to *close the clinic.*

Picketing will definitely be resisted by the abortionist. Therefore, it must be done within legal bounds. Acquire the necessary permit from local authorities and avoid labeling abortionists, by name, as murderers or the like. Such labeling has resulted in libel and slander suits and is not necessary (though true).

Some, like Joan and Miriam Andrews, believe it is their duty to sit in the doors of abortion clinics. The Andrews sisters have been arrested numerous times and have suffered jail sentences and even personal injury (such as broken bones) because of their protests. This type of activity will definitely result in criminal charges and convictions. Thus, those who go beyond legal picketing and resort to sit-ins and the like must be prepared to suffer the consequences. However, picketing is legal and requires only a commitment of time.

These alternatives should be done simultaneously. For example, a church that operates a pregnancy crisis center can also organize picketing. At the same time, Christians in the churches can be involved in political and legislative efforts.

Simply put, the church must protect those caught within

the razorlike clutches of the abortionists. If not, there will be judgment and little hope for evangelism or other freedoms. As 1 Peter 4:17 makes clear, "the time has come for judgment, and it must begin first among God's own children" *(The Living Bible)*.

Priority Two: The Traditional Family

From antiquity the family has served as the basic building block of free societies. Likewise, we find a strong emphasis on the high estate of parenthood in history. As William Barclay writes, "Wherever we turn in the ancient world, to Judaism, to Greece or to Rome, we find the insistence that parents must be honored and obeyed. When we turn to Christianity we find the same demand."[11]

One of the few exceptions to this historical rule has been the contemporary era. Contempt of the family goes hand in hand with contempt for religion and morality. The breakdown of the faith is also the breakdown of the family.

Contempt for the family is readily illustrated by the proliferation and easy access to pornography in this country. Pornography is a very subtle attack on the family. It reduces man and woman, husband and wife, mother and father to their genitals. It totally depersonalizes people. Women, especially, are portrayed more as things than as human beings.

Instead of being an expression of love, sex becomes a source of immediate gratification and eventually a form of manipulation. We see this in the current problem with the heavy use of children in prostitution.[12]

Pornography makes sex, one of the most private acts imaginable, public. Sex, in effect, becomes a public property. Naturally, what is public will eventually be linked with the state.

We see in history that statism and the rise of pornography go hand in hand. Thus, under an authoritarian state there is no distinction between private and public matters. "The only person who is still a private individual in Germany," boasted Robert Ley, a member of the Nazi hierarchy, after several years of Nazi rule, "is somebody who is asleep."[13]

Pornography has a denigrating effect on the psyche of a people. It eventually creates a servitude mentality. The Goncourt brothers, who studied the rise of pornography in early France, have written: "Pornographic literature serves a Bas-Empire . . . one tames a people as one tames lions, by masturbation."[14]

Laws have not stopped pornography. The last century has seen more legislation against pornography than any previous era has, and yet pornography has increased in its production and consumption.

The only way pornography can be curtailed is through a moral and spiritual revitalization of the people. And this will not happen until the family, the chief progenitor of morality and religion, regains its strength.

Totalitarians, however, hate the family because it is the basic thesis of all totalitarians that man's first loyalty must be to the state, whereas the Christian family's first allegiance is to the Creator. The totalitarian, therefore, seeks to abolish the family. Lenin said, "No nation can be free when half of the population is enslaved in the kitchen."[15]

As a result, the Communist state abolished the family as a legal entity until 1936. The family since then has merely been a legal breeding ground for the state. Moreover, women in the Soviet Union occupy heavy labor jobs and are mere slaves to the state.

In this country the family has not yet been abolished, but it is well on its way to a slow demise. There is hope for the family, however, if Christians take responsibility over their own families. This means Christians must take a hard look at what they are doing at home.

Christians can evangelize the world, but if they are neglecting their family in the process then, at least personally, their work is for nought. Evangelization and love for your fellow-creature starts at home.

The family should be the center of Christian life. No other institution (including the church) or activity should get in the way of family life.

A family is built upon human relationships. It takes effort on the part of parents to develop relationships with their children. It means taking *time* with children, reading aloud to them, playing with them, working with them, shopping with them, and so forth. This is all relationship building.

Children are the living messages we send to a time we will

not see. They are the combined images of their parents. They must, therefore, be molded with love and compassion.

Children must be guarded and protected but not shielded altogether from reality. Reality, like strong medicine though, must come in small doses. As we saw from our discussion of television, too much too soon obliterates the distinctions between children and adults.

Television, besides consuming precious time, invades the privacy of the home. It almost always teaches an ethic that runs contrary to the foundation of the traditional family. It is, then, a very subtle (although sometimes overt) attack on the family.

What should we do with it? Malcolm Muggeridge offers one solution: "I think the best thing to do is not to look at television, and to that end, I have, as has been said, disposed of my set."[16]

It is Muggeridge's opinion, as well as others', that television is a medium that cannot be much improved. It is a medium doomed to mediocrity.

Although I tend to agree with this, I believe that Christians must participate in the real world. They should not altogether deprive their children of a cultural reality such as television. Disposing of the television set will not make it disappear. Monitoring it can in large part tame it.

The obvious answer is "very, very" selective and limited viewing. This will, of course, not prevent bad material from seeping into your children's heads. It will, however, provide you the opportunity to educate them on what to watch. This means parents, if at all possible, should watch programs with their children. If questions arise, they can then be answered. If parents cannot do this, they should watch one episode of each show and approve it *before* their children watch the show.

These principles also apply to "Christian" programs. Because of its manipulative nature, some Christian programming is not healthy for adults or children (any more than secular programming).

Working on the remedies above will improve a family. However, a family will not work if it does not follow the biblical design set forth in Ephesians 5:21-23.

A true family functions from a hierarchical design. Ephesians 5:22-25 states:

Wives, submit yourselves unto your own husbands, as unto the Lord. For the husband is the head of the wife, even as Christ is the head of the church: and he is the Saviour of the body. Therefore as the church is subject unto Christ, so let the wives be to their own husbands in every thing. Husbands, love your wives, even as Christ also loved the church, and gave himself for it. (AV)

The principles set forth here are clear. The male is to act as the leader of the family. The wife submits to this leadership, not out of fear of her husband or because she is inferior to him, but out of her respect for Christ.

"Submission," then, does not mean enslavement. It is the "yielded, intelligent, humble obedience to an ordained authority. Christ was the ultimate example of submission. Throughout His time on earth, He submitted Himself to the will of the Father."[17]

Those who refer to submission by a wife to a loving husband as "slavery" often find themselves in a contradictory position. In fact, *Cosmopolitan* editor Helen Gurley Brown in *Having It All* refers to married women who stay at home as "drones."[18] While opposing marital submission, these people seem eager to expand the power of the state (and the courts) while submitting themselves and the entire society to state control.

Modern men have been feminized, and modern women have been masculinized. Sexual roles have been reversed. This, as George Gilder notes, will result in what he terms "sexual suicide."[19]

Men must become men again and regain their leadership role in the family. The effective father is a leader, a role model.

The family is much like a classroom. The parents, as teachers, must be effective role models. A culture will mirror what is taught by the parents in the family.

If we are to have leaders for tomorrow, then the fathers of today must be leaders in the family classroom. The modern lamentations concerning the loss of leaders in this country can be traced back to a breakdown in leadership as taught in the family.

The wife plays a very important part in supporting the leadership role of the husband. This is strategic because one of man's greatest needs is for respect. The way a man can be hurt the most is by being rejected publicly or privately by his wife. This, too, is part of the loving submission process. If the wife refuses to submit to her husband, their children probably will also refuse.

As discussed in Chapter Six, one of the major reasons for the breakdown of the family is the mother's working outside the home. *Christians need to ponder this issue carefully in light of its damaging effect.*

Mothers working outside the home have necessitated day care centers. This means that someone other than the parents are serving as parents. Deborah Fallows, writing in *Newsweek*, shows the danger in this:

> I think there is a danger of being too comforted, too reassured about putting our children in others' care for the major portion of the day. We risk imparting a message about families that ultimately hurts all working parents, but especially those who have to work. In saying that a parent's duties are largely replaceable, we put them on the same plane of importance as household chores. We are suggesting that working parents can buy a parent-substitute as easily as they can buy a frozen dinner.[20]

In addition to the husband being the leader of the family, he is also to be a compassionate lover of his wife. Ephesians 5:25 is very clear: "Husbands, love your wives, even as Christ also loved the church, and gave himself for it."

How does Christ love the church? With a sacrificial, giving, compassionate love. A husband's love for his wife should be similar.

This places the wife in a high estate. Thus, we see the practice, for example, of men opening doors for women. Such acts have roots in Christianity and, more specifically, Ephesians 5.

In addition to being the lover and the leader for his wife, the husband needs to be a good father to his children. Fathers represent God. They should reflect, therefore, as closely as possible, the Creator.

The family is not going to revive overnight. It will take work. It will be painful to accomplish because so many of the familial roots have been unplugged.

However, it must be done. And it must be based upon Christian principles, because they are the only sure foundation for life.

Priority Three: The Church and the Private School

The church and the private school are discussed together

since they are often locked together and because they represent the last remnants of private action that operate relatively free from state involvement.

The church faces two threats simultaneously. First, there is the problem of the church becoming so closely tied to conservative politics that the distinctions between Christian and non-Christian political motives and actions become blurred.

As there is yet no Christian mind, neither is there any true Christian political agenda. Christians have simply failed to develop a distinctively Christian political strategy.

There is much to learn from political involvement by Christians in conservative politics. And Christians must remain active in the political arena. However, until a Christian political strategy is developed, Christians must be mindful that they not be manipulated by interest groups or a state that pushes a conservative line.

In his book *Tortured for Christ* Richard Wurmbrand recounts the Communist takeover of Rumania in the early 1940s:

> Once the communists came to power, they skillfully used the means of seduction toward the Church. The language of love and the language of seduction are the same. The one who wishes a girl for a wife and the one who wishes her for a night in order to throw her away afterward, both say, "I love you." Jesus has told us to distinguish the language of seduction from the language of love, and to know the wolves clad in sheepskin from the real sheep.[21]

The problem was, as Wurmbrand writes: "When the communists came to power thousands of priests, pastors, and ministers did not know how to distinguish the two voices."[22] As a consequence, "Orthodox and Protestant church leaders competed with each other in yielding to communism. An Orthodox bishop put the hammer and sickle on his robes and asked his priests not to call him anymore 'Your Grace,' but 'Comrade Bishop.' "[23]

The second threat is the increasing involvement and interference of the state in the church and her ministries. However, a note of caution is appropriate.

Although the church should fight state regulation of the church, the battles she fights must be chosen with care. In other words, the church must draw the battle lines at the most strategic places.

Drawing the line on content control and the inherent right of the church to exist is biblical. Intrusive content control by the state, in the form of approving or disapproving the content of the teaching of God's truth, is prohibited by the Bible. The apostles were forbidden to "teach in this [Christ's] name." Peter replied to the Sanhedrin, "We must obey God rather than men" (Acts 5:28, 29).

State control that threatens the inherent right of the church to exist is also objectionable. This would include such things as government attempts to define what is a true church. If the state proclaims by way of government definition that a church cannot or should not legally exist, then such government actions should be resisted.

Some, however, have not been so wise to fight the battle over intrusive content control issues. They have, for example, contested in court the state's authority to require health and safety regulations in churches and Christian schools. This is a losing battle. It also expends much time and money fighting something that churches should be doing anyway (that is, have safe buildings). Thus, as a matter of tactics it is wise for churches and Christian schools not to struggle against *reasonable* state health and safety regulations. It is really a side issue.

A great danger facing the Christian school movement and other Christian causes is ill-advised lawsuits that generally establish bad precedents. Court battles that are sure to set bad case precedents must be avoided because when the case arises worth fighting, all the losing precedents will be cited against the church or Christian school by the state. It is a needless burden to bear by attorneys defending Christians and others.

Thus, the costs (in terms of money, time spent, energy used, and bad precedents set) must be counted before going to court. This means that lawsuits should be fought over basics and not incidentals.

In light of the issues, churches should have two immediate priorities. First, they must educate their people on the issues and the proper response to the issues. We must be apologists for the faith, and that necessitates being informed.

Second, the church and Christian schools must prepare for the continuing legal and legislative battles. Watchdog committees should be formed in local churches, composed of individual members, to monitor legislation affecting the exercise of the faith.

Local church associations and national church fellowships should also establish legal defense funds. Christians must be cognizant of the fact that lawsuits have high costs in time and money. A major constitutional case today will, if it is handled properly, cost many thousands of dollars. You get what you pay for, and competent legal counsel and representation will cost money.

All this translates into organized, strategic jousting while being wary of the pitfalls laid before the church. This is essential if the church is to remain free to operate without state control.

Priority Four: Freedom in the Public Arena

Our secular society quite logically and consistently is trying to close the door to the freedom of religious expression in public places. This censorship is most visible in the public schools where, as of this writing, many Christian teachers and students are severely restricted in terms of free speech.

The right to exercise one's religion was once an assumed freedom in the public schools. However, because of the great exodus of Christians from the educational professions, the reins of education were grasped and have for years been controlled by the secularists.

If religious people do not regain their right to free speech in the public schools and other public places, then religion will be totally *privatized,* much as it is in countries like the Soviet Union. There "freedom" of religion is allowed only in a controlled church.

The United States Supreme Court has upheld the right of Christians to meet and worship on university campuses. In schizophrenic fashion, however, this same right currently is denied to high school students. Thus, Christian students and teachers are not free to meet on school property on an equal basis with others. A priority here is to establish the legal precedent to allow such a freedom.

There must also be legal precedent strengthening the Christian teacher's right, at the least, to express his or her honest opinion on the Creator or Christ. This right, too, is presently in jeopardy.

If these precedents and freedoms are not forthcoming, those Christians in public education are faced with two possibilities. Either they leave the system or resist. Again, resistance and civil disobedience will result in penalties and perpetrators of such must prepare to suffer the consequences. Consequences could range from the firing of a teacher to suspension of students. These penalties should be met with lawsuits in carefully selected test cases.

Millions of children sit entombed in an educational system that, in most instances, omits any serious reference to God. These children need to hear the truth. Thus, even those Christians who disagree with public education must seek to evangelize the public schools.

We should also fight for the right of students to have voluntary prayer in public schools. It must be truly voluntary and free of coercion. For example, if students want to meet for prayer over the lunch hour or before school begins, or to read the Bible or discuss religion, this should be their right.

However, voluntary means voluntary. Christians should be very careful of supporting any government-composed prayers which, although they appear voluntary, require student participation (even if nonparticipating students are exempted).

Make no mistake about it: enrollment may be declining in the public schools, but they will be around for some time. If the church fails to have a significant witness in public education, where most of the next generation will be trained, then the next generation will inevitably be more hostile to Christianity than this generation. That could spell disaster.

Priority Five: Those Oppressed for Their Faith

"I tremble," Richard Wurmbrand writes, "for Western Christians who don't help their persecuted brethren."[24]

The West watched as the Communist bloc gobbled up one country after another. As Afghanistan and Poland fell, we watched with bewilderment.

Within these countries and others behind the Iron Curtain, thousands of Christians are persecuted and imprisoned for their religious beliefs. We have missions to some of these people. But have we visited the sick and the needy in prison? Christ said,

"Inasmuch as ye have done it unto one of the least of these my brethren, ye have done it unto me" (Matthew 25:40).

Western Christians simply have not met the needs of those oppressed by foreign tyrants. However, Moses demanded of Pharaoh and Jesus demanded of the prince of darkness, Let my people go! Not so with Christians in the West. Brother Andrew writes:

> Christians in the West are the silent majority, making no such demand. Spineless, colorless, passive individuals, we as the silent majority form the bridge over which the world of corruption, revolution and hatred passes unhindered. Passes over to corrode and curse the lives of the rising generations. And in what we call democracy there is no force that can possibly stop it, except the power of God.[25]

What Iron Curtain Christians go through has, like abortion in this country, been partially hidden from American eyes. The persecution, however, is horrible. "What the communists have done to Christians," Richard Wurmbrand notes, "surpasses any possibility of human understanding."[26]

In *Tortured for Christ,* Wurmbrand describes the persecution:

> A pastor by the name of Florescu was tortured with red-hot iron pokers and with knives. He was beaten very badly. Then starving rats were driven into his cell through a large pipe. He could not sleep, but had to defend himself all the time. If he rested a moment, the rats would attack him. . . .
>
> We Christians were put in wooden boxes only slightly larger than we were. This left no room to move. Dozens of sharp nails were driven into every side of the box, with their razor-sharp points sticking into the box. While we stood perfectly still, it was all right. We were forced to stand in these boxes for endless hours. But when we became fatigued and swayed with tiredness, the nails would go into our bodies. If we moved or twitched a muscle—there were the horrible nails. . . .
>
> I have seen communists torturing Christians and the faces of the torturers shone with rapturous joy. They cried out while torturing the Christians, "We are the devil."[27]

This is merely a sample of what is happening to people in these totalitarian states. What can we do for them?

First, we must be in continual prayer for the oppressed. Prayer should be directed at their peace of mind but also for freedom from their oppressors.

Second, we must financially support organizations that are smuggling materials into these countries.

Third, we need more missionaries to go behind the Iron Curtain and visit and speak with these people to encourage them. Moreover, attorneys should make themselves available to defend these people. And Christians should contribute to make possible this legal aid.

Fourth, we should work at every level to undermine totalitarian governments. We should protest when our government supports countries like the Soviet Union with technology. Unfortunately our country has, so to speak, kept some of the totalitarian states in the business of persecution and tyranny.

We should speak loudly and clearly, using every political and media means at our disposal for these oppressed people. If we cannot do these minimal things, then those oppressed for their faith will languish in the dungeons. And we will surely be judged for our omissions (Matthew 25:45, 46).

Standing Boldly

The story of King Hezekiah illustrates very well the spirit of our age. After Isaiah had pronounced a series of devastating curses upon Hezekiah (including a foreign state's carrying away his sons and making them eunuchs, 2 Kings 20) Hezekiah responded by saying: "Good is the word of the Lord which thou hast spoken. And he said, Is it not good, if peace and truth be in my days?" (verse 19). In other words, as long as Hezekiah could live his own life in peace and security, he didn't really concern himself about the terror that was coming upon future generations (including his own children).

Francis A. Schaeffer has shown that ours is an age characterized by two basic values: personal peace and affluence. These result in a willingness to compromise most everything in order to keep these values intact.

Aleksandr Solzhenitsyn speaks of how the Russian people would kneel inside the door of their apartments, pressing their ears to listen when the KGB came at midnight to arrest a neighbor. He says that if all the people would have come out and driven off the officers, sheer public opinion would have demoralized the effort to subdue a free people. But their own personal peace was more important.

Many of those who press for a secular society, free of the Christian ethic, know very well where their philosophy leads. Existentialist Jean-Paul Sartre, quoting Fyodor Dostoevsky, writes:

> Dostoievski said, "If God didn't exist, everything [murder, robbery, rape, etc.] would be possible." That is the very starting point of Existentialism. Indeed, everything is permissible if God does not exist.[28]

Secularizing agents such as the American Civil Liberties Union know very well what they are doing. When ACLU attorneys threaten or sue public school districts in the name of freedom to stop a child from voluntarily praying, they are not standing for freedom. The ACLU is repressing a whole segment of society—religious people—as if it were an appendage of the secular state.

Oppression and fear represent the spirit of our age, and they lead to totalitarianism. Christians, however, must not allow the spirit of this age to dominate their thinking. It must be the other way around. We must stand boldly in our secular era or be controlled by a cruel taskmaster.

There is hope if Christians once again become involved in our culture and society in a meaningful way. Christians have too long been absent from involvement in the significant issues of our times.

In the context of the slide toward authoritarianism, we must, without fear, proclaim the principles of Christ. Specifically, they are: If one serves God absolutely he cannot so serve the state; and if one, being created in the image of God, loves his neighbor he will seek to serve his fellowman (Matthew 22:37-39). He will also protect his fellowman's life, family, and humanity in the face of the secularistic authoritarian state.

Thus, it may be said that the principles of Christ's moral code *demand* reverence for God and respect for the dignity of man. William Barclay writes that without these principles "society can become a place in which, as in a totalitarian state, men are looked on as things and not as persons. Reverence for God and respect for man can never be separated from each other."[29]

The authoritarian state fears the principles of Christ because if practiced with compassion, they will deter and lead to the abolition of repressive states.

Human life, the family, the church, and our freedoms are sacred. They are endowed by God. Even the state must be made to realize this.

If the state refuses, then Christians must put their faith to the test and stand and protest invasions of our sacred freedoms. A real faith results in works. And we who perceive the very real threat in the present situation must work diligently and quickly if we are to be the witnesses Christ has commanded us to be.

NOTES

Chapter 1: A Time of Parenthesis

1. As quoted by Richard Wurmbrand, *Tortured for Christ* (Glendale, CA: Diane Books, 1967), p. 80.
2. Alvin Toffler, *The Third Wave* (New York: Morrow, 1980).
3. B. F. Skinner, *Beyond Freedom and Dignity* (New York: Knopf, 1971).
4. Joel Greenberg, "B. F. Skinner Now Sees Little Hope for the World's Salvation," *New York Times* (September 15, 1981), p. C-1.
5. Malcolm Muggeridge, *The End of Christendom* (Grand Rapids, MI: Eerdmans, 1980), p. 17.
6. George Orwell, *Nineteen Eighty-Four* (New York: Harcourt, Brace and World, 1949), p. 270.
7. Jacques Ellul, *The Political Illusion* (New York: Vintage Press, 1972), p. 9.
8. Bertram Gross, *Friendly Fascism: The New Face of Power in America* (New York: M. Evans, 1980), p. 124.
9. *Op. cit.*, Ellul, p. 10 (emphasis supplied).
10. *Op. cit.*, Gross, p. 3.
11. Kenneth Dolbeare, "Alternatives to the New Fascism," paper delivered at the American Political Science Association, September 1976, as quoted by *op. cit.*, Gross, p. 2.
12. *Ibid.*, p. 3.
13. *Ibid.*
14. Francis A. Schaeffer, *How Should We Then Live?* (Old Tappan, NJ: Revell, 1976), p. 228 (emphasis in original). As Schaeffer writes:

> What of tomorrow? In the United States, for example, a manipulative authoritarian government could come from the administrative side or from the legislative side. A public official in the United States serving at the highest level has wisely said, "Legislative dictatorship is no better than executive tyranny." And one would have to add that with the concept of variable law and with the courts making law, it could come from the judicial side as well. The Supreme Court has the final voice in regard to both administrative and legislative actions, and with the concept of variable law the judicial side could become more and more the center of power. This could be called "the imperial judiciary. . . ." (*Ibid.*, pp. 244, 245.)

15. Kevin P. Phillips, *Post-Conservative America: People, Politics, and Ideology in a Time of Crisis* (New York: Random House, 1981), p. 164.
16. Franky Schaeffer, *A Time for Anger: The Myth of Neutrality* (Westchester, IL: Crossway Books, 1982), p. 26.
17. Roland Huntford, *The New Totalitarians* (New York: Stein and Day, 1972), p. 11.
18. *Op. cit.*, Schaeffer, p. 245.
19. William Irwin Thompson, " 'What's Past is Prologue,' The Past—What's That?", *New York Times* (June 10, 1976), p. 37.
20. *Ibid.*
21. Aldous Huxley, *Brave New World* (1939) (New York: Bantam Books, 1968), p. xii.

Chapter 2: On the Road to Auschwitz

1. William Shirer, *The Rise and Fall of the Third Reich* (New York: Simon & Schuster, 1960), pp. 69, 70.
2. Leonard Peikoff, *The Ominous Parallels: The End of Freedom in America* (Briarcliff, NY: Stein and Day, 1982), p. 5 (emphasis in original).
3. Michael Novak, *The Spirit of Democratic Capitalism* (New York: American Enterprise Institute/Simon and Schuster, 1982), p. 183.
4. Georg Wilhelm Friedrich Hegel, trans. T. M. Knox, *Philosophy of Right* (London: Oxford Press, 1967), p. 241.
5. Georg Wilhelm Friedrich Hegel, trans. J. Sibree, *The Philosophy of History*, rev. ed. (New York: Colonial Press, 1900), p. 39.
6. *Op. cit.*, Hegel, *Philosophy of Right*, p. 156.
7. Adolf Hitler, *Mein Kampf* (1925) (New York: Houghton, Mifflin, 1971), pp. 214, 215.
8. Aurel Kolnai, *The War Against the West* (New York: Viking Press, 1938), p. 59.
9. *Op. cit.*, Peikoff, p. 8 (emphasis in original).
10. *Ibid.*
11. *Ibid.*
12. Robert E. Clark, *Darwin: Before and After* (London: Paternoster, 1948), p. 115.
13. Charles Darwin, *The Origin of the Species by Means of Natural Selection or the Preservation of Favoured Races in the Struggle for Life* (1859) (New York: Oxford University Press, 1963).
14. Stephen Jay Gould, *The Mismeasure of Man* (New York: W. W. Norton, 1981).
15. Arthur Keith, *Evolution and Ethics* (New York: G. P. Putnam's Sons, 1949), p. 230.
16. *Op. cit.*, Peikoff, p. 55.
17. *Ibid.*, p. 6.
18. N. H. Baynes, ed., *The Speeches of Adolf Hitler, 1922-39*, Vol. I (London: Oxford University Press, 1942), pp. 871, 872.

19. Crane Brinston, John B. Christopher and Robert Lee Wolff, *A History of Civilization*, Vol. 2, 2nd ed. (Englewood Cliffs, NJ: Prentice-Hall, 1963), p. 484.
20. Julian Huxley, "Evolution and Genetics," *What is Science?*, J. R. Newman, ed. (New York: Simon & Schuster, 1955), pp. 272-278.
21. Jon Barton and John Whitehead, *Schools on Fire* (Wheaton, IL: Tyndale House, 1980), p. 65.
22. *Op. cit.*, Peikoff, p. 130.
23. *Ibid.*
24. *Ibid.*, p. 291.
25. Dewey was a signer of *Humanist Manifesto I*. Its preface proclaims:

> In every field of human activity, the vital movement is now in the direction of a candid and explicit humanism. In order that religious humanism may be better understood we, the undersigned, desire to make certain affirmations which we believe the facts of our contemporary life demonstrate.
>   Today man's larger understanding of the universe, his scientific achievements, and his deeper appreciation of brotherhood, have created a situation which requires a new statement of the means and purposes of religion. . . . [I]t is . . . obvious that any religion that can hope to be a synthesizing and dynamic force today must be shaped for the needs of this age. To establish such a religion is a major necessity of the present.

26. John Dewey, *Characters and Events: Popular Essays in Social and Political Philosophy*, Vol. 2 (New York: Holt, 1929), p. 515.
27. Newton Edwards, *The Courts and the Public Schools*, 3rd ed. (Chicago: University of Chicago Press, 1971), pp. 23, 24.
28. David A. Diamond, "The First Amendment and Public Schools: The Case Against Judicial Intervention," *Texas Law Review* 59 (1981) 477, 498.
29. *Ibid.*
30. *City of Louisville v. Commonwealth*, 134 Ky. 488, 121 S.W. 411, 411-12 (1909).
31. *McCollum v. Board of Education*, 333 U.S. 203, 216, 217 (1948).
32. *Brown v. Board of Education*, 347 U.S. 483, 493 (1954).
33. Richard M. Hunt, "No-Fault Guilt-Free History," *New York Times* (February 16, 1976), p. 19.
34. C. S. Lewis, *God in the Dock* (Grand Rapids, Mich.: Eerdmans, 1971), p. 288.

Chapter 3: Some Ominous Parallels

1. Kevin P. Phillips, *Post-Conservative America: People, Politics, and Ideology in a Time of Crisis* (New York: Random House, 1981), p. 157.
2. *Ibid.*
3. *Ibid.*
4. Alvin Toffler, *The Third Wave* (New York: Morrow, 1980), p. 26.
5. John Naisbitt, *Megatrends: Ten New Directions Transforming Our Lives* (New York: Warner Books, 1982), p. 18.
6. *Ibid.*, pp. 64, 65.

7. *Op. cit.*, Phillips, p. 158. Also see Kevin P. Phillips, "A Sense of Inevitability," King Features Syndicate (May 22, 1979).

8. *Op. cit.*, Phillips, *Post-Conservative America*, p. 159.

9. Daniel J. Danelski and Joseph S. Tulchin, eds., *The Autobiographical Notes of Charles Evans Hughes* (Cambridge: Harvard University Press, 1973), p. 143.

10. The Supreme Court's distortion of the Constitution by way of interpretation is thoroughly analyzed in my book, *The Second American Revolution* (Elgin, IL: David C. Cook, 1982).

11. Marshall McLuhan, "Cybernation and Culture," *The Social Impact of Cybernetics* (New York: Simon & Schuster, 1966), p. 99.

12. Robert Bork, "The Struggle Over the Role of the Court," *National Review* (September 17, 1982), p. 138.

13. *Ibid.*

14. *Ibid.*

15. *Ibid.*

16. For example, see Blake Fleetwood, "The Tax Police: Trampling Citizens' Rights," *Saturday Review* (May 1980), pp. 33-36; Michael Satchell, "Fear the IRS," *Parade* (April 12, 1981), pp. 4-9.

17. *Op. cit.*, Naisbitt, p. 103.

18. *Ibid.*

19. *American Political Report* (August 17, 1979), p. 3. An extensive study recently showed that slightly less than two-fifths of the public believe that America's major national problems can be solved through traditional American politics. *The Connecticut Mutual Life Report on American Values in the '80s: The Impact of Belief*, Hartford, CT: Connecticut Mutual Life Insurance Company (1981), p. 202.

20. *Op. cit.*, Phillips, p. 160.

21. *Ibid.*

22. *Ibid.*

23. Sterling Segrave, *Yellow Rain* (New York: M. Evans, 1981).

24. *Op. cit.*, Phillips, p. 164.

Chapter 4: The Loss of Traditional Values

1. B. F. Skinner, *Beyond Freedom and Dignity* (New York: Knopf, 1971), p. 180.

2. Humanism as used in this book does not refer to humanitarianism or the study of the humanities. The term, used here in its "wider, more prevalent way means Man beginning from himself, with no knowledge except what he himself can discover and no standards outside of himself. In this view Man is the measure of all things, as the Enlightenment expressed it." Francis A. Schaeffer, *A Christian Manifesto* (Westchester, IL: Crossway Books, 1981), p. 24.

3. Secularism is the belief that morality is based solely in regard to the temporal well-being of mankind to the exclusion of any belief in God, a supreme being, or a future eternity. It is the view that consideration of the present well-being

of mankind should predominate over supernatural or religous considerations in political affairs. See James Hitchcock, *What Is Secular Humanism?* (Ann Arbor, MI: Servant Books, 1982).

4. Leonard Peikoff, *The Ominous Parallels: The End of Freedom in America* (Briarcliff Manor, NY: Stein and Day, 1982), p. 182.

5. *Ibid.*

6. H. R. Rookmaaker, *Modern Art and the Death of a Culture* (Downers Grove, IL: InterVarsity Press, 1970), p. 220.

7. *Ibid.,* p. 188-190.

8. Glen O'Brien, "Notes on the Neon Nihilists," *High Times* (November 1980), p. 56.

9. Laura Coleman and David Waters, "Controversy Over Nazis Raises Fears," *The Commercial Appeal* (November 17, 1982), p. A-1. One should not be shocked at the influx of Nazi ideas in this country in light of recent research which indicates that many Nazis, some of whom were known murderers, were brought into this country during and after World War II by the United States government. See John Loftus, *The Belarus Secret* (New York: Knopf, 1982).

10. Spencer Vibbert, "Punk, Boston Style," *Boston Globe Magazine* (March 2, 1980), p. 8.

11. "Europe's Anti-Semitism," *Newsweek* (August 23, 1982), p. 35.

12. Alison Muscatine, "Cross-Burnings, Anti-Semitic Acts Increasing Here," *Washington Post* (November 22, 1982), p. A-1.

13. Kevin P. Phillips, *Post-Conservative America: People, Politics, and Ideology in a Time of Crisis* (New York: Random House, 1981), p. 159.

14. John Naisbitt, *Megatrends: Ten New Directions Transforming Our Lives* (New York: Warner Books, 1982), p. 40.

15. *Ibid.*

16. Swami Vivekananda, *Inspired Talks* (New York: Ramakrishna Vivekananda Center, 1958), p. 218.

17. Brooks Alexander, "The Rise of Cosmic Humanism: What Is Religion?", *SCP Journal* (Winter 1981-82), p. 2.

18. Dina Ingber, "Brain Breathing," *Science Digest* (June 1981), p. 111. Also see Mary Long, "Visions of a New Faith," *Science Digest* (November 1981), p. 36.

19. Alvin Toffler, *The Third Wave* (New York: Morrow, 1980), p. 391.

20. *Ibid.,* p. 392.

21. *Op. cit.,* Alexander, p. 4.

22. Harvey Cox, *The Secular City* (New York: Macmillan, 1965), p. 18.

23. *Op. cit.,* Alexander, p. 2.

24. Dusty Skylar, *God and Beasts: Nazis and the Occult* (New York: Crowell, 1977).

25. Gary North, *None Dare Call It Witchcraft* (New Rochelle, NY: Arlington House, 1976), pp. 43-49. Also see Sheila Ostrander and Lynn Schroeder, *Psychic Discoveries Behind the Iron Curtain* (New York: Bantam Books, 1970).

26. *Op. cit.,* North, p. 44.

27. J. S. Conway, *The Nazi Persecution of the Church, 1933-45* (New York: Basic Books, 1968), p. 334.

28. John W. Whitehead, "The Boston Tea Party 1982?" *Christianity Today* (November 12, 1982), pp. 28-30.
29. *Op. cit.*, Conway, p. 335.
30. *Ibid.*
31. See Francis A. Schaeffer, *A Christian Manifesto* (Westchester, IL: Crossway Books, 1981); John W. Whitehead, *The Second American Revolution* (Elgin, IL: David C. Cook, 1982); Franky Schaeffer, *A Time for Anger* (Westchester, IL: Crossway Books, 1982).
32. Peter Matheson, *The Third Reich and the Christian Churches* (Grand Rapids, MI: Eerdmans, 1981), pp. 26, 27.
33. *Op. cit.*, Conway, p. 336.
34. William Barclay, *The Ten Commandments for Today* (Grand Rapids, MI: Eerdmans, 1973), p. 94.
35. *Ibid.*
36. Jacques Ellul, *The Political Illusion* (1967) (New York: Vintage Books, 1972), p. 21.

Chapter 5: The Devaluation of Human Life

1. Sharon Begley, "Nature's Baby Killers," *Newsweek* (September 6, 1982), p. 79.
2. *Colorado Springs Gazette Telegraph* (December 16, 1981), p. 9-C.
3. As quoted in A. E. Wilder-Smith, *He Who Thinks Has To Believe* (Minneapolis: Bethany House, 1981), p. 71. Cf. David H. Hubel, "The Brain," *Scientific American* (September 1979), pp. 45-52.
4. *Ibid.*
5. As quoted by Michael Schwartz, "Abortion: The Nazi Connection," *Catholic League Newsletter* (August 1978), p. 1.
6. *Ibid.*
7. *Ibid.*
8. *Ibid.*, p. 2.
9. Allan Chase, *The Legacy of Malthus: The Social Costs of the New Scientific Racism* (New York: Knopf, 1976), p. 349.
10. A thorough discussion of the factors involved in the decline of the sanctity of human life is provided by James Tunstead Burtchaell, *Rachael Weeping and Other Essays on Abortion* (Fairway, KS: Andrews and McMeel, 1982).
11. James Tunstead Burtchaell, "The Holocaust and Abortion," Supplement to *Catholic League Newsletter*, Vol. 9, No. 11.
12. *Buck v. Bell*, 274 U.S. 200 (1927).
13. *Ibid.*, p. 207.
14. As quoted in Richard Hertz, *Chance and Symbol* (Chicago: University of Chicago Press, 1948), p. 107.
15. Stephen J. Gould, *The Mismeasure of Man* (New York: W. W. Norton, 1981), p. 335.
16. *Ibid.*

17. *Ibid.*
18. *Roe v Wade,* 410 U.S. 113 (1973).
19. *Op. cit.,* Burtchaell, *Catholic League Newsletter,* p. 2.
20. *International Life Times* (November 7, 1980), p. 9.
21. *Ibid.*
22. Thomas J. Marzen, "Aborted Babies Born at Hospital with 'Model' Eugenics Program," *National Right To Life News* (May 20, 1982), p. 1.
23. *Ibid.,* p. 8.
24. *Op. cit.,* Burtchaell, *Catholic League Newsletter,* p. 2.
25. *Ibid.*
26. *Ibid.,* pp. 2, 3.
27. *Ibid.,* p. 3.
28. *Ibid.,* p. 4.
29. *Ibid.*
30. John W. Whitehead, *The Second American Revolution* (Elgin, IL: David C. Cook, 1982), p. 67.
31. "Post-Abortion Fetal Study Stirs Storm," *Medical World News* (June 8, 1973), p. 21.
32. "Philosopher Proposes Euthanasia for Severely Disabled Infants," *Newport News Daily Press* (January 10, 1982), p. A-12.
33. *Ibid.*
34. *Ibid.*
35. "Doctor Sees Trend Not to Resuscitate," *Washington Post* (June 12, 1982), p. A-4. Also see "Doctor's Dilemma: Treat or Let Die," *U.S. News and World Report* (December 6, 1982), p. 53.
36. *Op. cit.,* Burtchaell, *Catholic League Newsletter,* p. 5.
37. Leonard Peikoff, *The Ominous Parallels: The End of Freedom in America* (New York: Stein and Day, 1982), pp. 269, 270.
38. *Ibid.,* p. 270.
39. *Op. cit.,* Burtchaell, *Catholic League Newsletter,* p. 6.
40. *Ibid.*
41. "Economy Cited by Many as Reason for Abortion," *Presbyterian Journal* (November 17, 1982), p. 5.
42. Bernard N. Nathanson, M.D. with Richard M. Ostling, *Aborting America* (Garden City, NY: Doubleday, 1979).
43. Lecture given by Dr. Bernard N. Nathanson at the Legislative Building, Albany, New York (March 17, 1981).
44. *Op. cit.,* Burtchaell, *Catholic League Newsletter,* p. 7.
45. *Ibid.*
46. Nick Thimmesch, "Fetuses and Cosmetics: The French Connection," *Los Angeles Times Syndicate* (1982).
47. *Ibid.*
48. *Ibid.*
49. *Ibid.*
50. *Ibid.*
51. *Ibid.*
52. Mark Gladstone, "Evidence Sought in Deaths of Fetuses," *Los Angeles Times* (February 7, 1982).

53. George F. Will, "Abortion Does Cause Pain to Its Victims," *Washington Post* (November 5, 1981), p. A-29. Recent research indicates that unborn children do experience many sensations, including pain. See Thomas Verny, M.D. with John Kelly, *The Secret Life of the Unborn Child* (New York: Summit Books, 1981).
54. "Court Affirms $178,000 for Va. Couple," *Washington Post* (May 1, 1982), p. B-2.
55. "Abortion Found Safer Than Giving Birth," *Washington Post* (July 9, 1982), p. A-2.

Chapter 6: The Decline of the Family

1. Sidney Abbott and Barbara Love, *Sappho Was a Right-On Woman: A Liberated View of Lesbianism* (New York: Stein and Day, 1972).
2. *New York Times Book Review* (February 25, 1973), p. 39.
3. *Ibid.*, pp. 39, 40.
4. Urie Bronfenbrenner, "The Disturbing Changes in the American Family," *Search* (State University of New York, Fall 1976); as reprinted in *The Journal of Christian Reconstruction*, IV (Winter 1977-78), p. 39.
5. *Ibid.*, p. 43.
6. *Ibid.*, p. 45.
7. John Naisbitt, *Megatrends: Ten New Directions Transforming Our Lives* (New York: Warner Books, 1982), p. 236. These trends are thoroughly analyzed by Lenore J. Weitzman, "Changing Families, Changing Laws," *Family Advocate* (Summer 1982), pp. 2-7, 40, 41. Also see "Death of the Family," *Newsweek* (January 17, 1983), pp. 26-28.
8. Alvin Toffler, *The Third Wave* (New York: Bantam Books, 1981), pp. 211, 212.
9. *Op. cit.*, Weitzman, p. 4 (emphasis in original).
10. *Op. cit.*, Naisbitt, p. 233. Among the Center's predictions for the year 1990:

> Husband-wife households with only one working spouse will account for only 14 percent of all households, as compared with 43 percent in 1960.
> Wives will contribute about 40 percent of family income, compared to about 25 percent now.
> At least thirteen separate types of households will eclipse the conventional family, including such categories as "female head, widowed, with children" and "male head, previously married, with children."
> More than a third of the couples first married in the 1970s will have divorced; more than a third of the children born in the 1970s will have spent part of their childhood living with a single parent (and emotional and financial consequences of this trend will be commensurately large).

Ibid., pp. 233, 234.
11. *Op. cit.*, Weitzman, p. 4. In 1970, 43 percent of the married couples did not have children in their home. By 1978, the proportion had risen to 48 percent. *Ibid.*
12. Cristine Russell, "Scientist's Review of '70s Abortions 'Largely Positive,'" *Washington Post* (March 19, 1982), p. A-11.

13. *Op. cit.*, Weitzman, p. 4.
14. *Ibid.*, p. 5.
15. *Ibid.*, p. 4.
16. *Ibid.*, p. 5.
17. As quoted in Aric Press, "Divorce American Style," *Newsweek* (January 10, 1983), p. 42.
18. *Op. cit.*, Weitzman, p. 5.
19. *Ibid.*
20. *Ibid.*, p. 6.
21. Spencer Rich, "Single-Parent Families Rise Dramatically," *Washington Post* (May 3, 1982), p. A-5. Also see Michael Marriott and Sara Rimer, "Adult-Oriented Washington Area Leads U.S. Life-Style Changes," *Washington Post* (November 7, 1982), p. A-1.
22. *Op. cit.*, Rich, p. A-5.
23. *Ibid.*
24. *Ibid.* "The Census Bureau reports that one-third of the nation's children live in homes without at least one of their biological parents." *Op. cit.*, Press, p. 42.
25. *Op. cit.*, Weitzman, p. 6.
26. *Ibid.*
27. *Ibid.*, p. 7.
28. *Ibid.*
29. *Ibid.*
30. *Ibid.*
31. *Ibid.*
32. *Ibid.*, p. 40. Weitzman disagrees with 1980 United States Census which indicates that there are about three million unmarried persons "sharing a household with an unrelated adult of the opposite sex." *Ibid.*
33. *Op. cit.*, Rich, p. A-5.
34. *Op. cit.*, Toffler, p. 215.
35. *Ibid.*, p. 212. Toffler's statistics are substantiated by a recent report by the United States Census Bureau. "Population of Singles Rising, Census Reports," *Washington Post* (October 19, 1981), p. A-16.
36. *Op. cit.*, Naisbitt, p. 233.
37. "Looking Ahead: Nine Top Women Eye the Future," *Working Women* (December 1982), p. 117.
38. George Gilder, *Sexual Suicide* (New York: Quadrangle Books, 1973), p. 15.
39. *Op. cit.*, Bronfenbrenner, p. 42.
40. Wendell R. Bird provides a thorough discussion of peer pressure in Note, "Freedom of Religion and Science Instruction in Public Schools," *Yale Law Journal* 87, (1976) 515, 532-536.
41. James Coleman, *The Adolescent Society* (New York: Free Press, 1971), p. 3 (emphasis in original).
42. Harry C. Bredemeier and Richard M. Stephenson, *The Analysis of Social Systems* (New York: Holt, Rinehart, and Winston, 1962), p. 119.
43. *Op. cit.*, Toffler, p. 213-216.

44. This number represented .0004 percent of the under-fifteen population of America. In that same year, 94,784 persons fifteen years and older were arrested for serious crimes, representing .0860 percent of the population fifteen years and older. Neil Postman, *The Disappearance of Childhood* (New York: Delacorte Press, 1982), p. 134.

45. This represented .2430 percent of the adult population. *Ibid.*

46. *Ibid.*

47. *Ibid.*, p. 135.

48. *Ibid.*, p. 85.

49. *Ibid.*, p. 75.

50. David Elkind, *The Hurried Child* (Reading, MA: Addison-Wesley, 1981), p. 73.

51. *Op. cit.*, Postman, p. 79.

52. Frank Mankiewicz and Joel Swendlow, *Remote Control* (New York: Ballantine, 1979), p. 17.

53. *Op. cit.*, Postman, p. 79.

54. *Op. cit.*, Elkind, p. 75-77.

55. *Op. cit.*, Postman, p. 137.

56. *Ibid.* (emphasis in original). See Stephanie Ventura, "Teenage Childbearing: United States, 1966-75," *The Monthly Vital Statistics Report*, a publication of the National Center for Health Statistics. It has also been noted that one in six American babies is now born out of wedlock, 50 percent more than a decade ago, and most to mothers past their teens, new government figures show. "One in Six U.S. Babies Born out of Wedlock," *Washington Post* (October 27, 1981), p. A-7.

57. *Op. cit.*, Postman, p. 137. Between 1956 and 1979, the percentage of ten to fourteen-year-olds suffering from gonorrhea increased threefold, from 17.7 per 100,000 population to 50.4. Roughly the same increase is found in the fifteen to nineteen-year-old group (from 415.7 per 100,000 to 1,211.4). *Ibid.*

58. *Ibid.*

59. See "Student Drug Use in America, 1975-1980," prepared by Lloyd Johnson, Jerald Bachman, and Patrick O'Malley of the University of Michigan Institute for Social Research. It is available from the National Institute on Drug Abuse, Rockville, Maryland 20857.

60. *Op. cit.*, Postman, pp. 134-142.

61. *Ibid.*, p. 139.

62. *Ibid.*, p. 85.

63. *Ibid.*, pp. 85, 86. "Our barbarians are home products indoctrinated at the public expense, urged on by the media systematically stage by stage, dismantling Christendom, depreciating and deprecating all its values." Malcolm Muggeridge, *The End of Christendom* (Grand Rapids, MI: Eerdmans, 1980), p. 17.

64. Margaret Mead, *Culture and Commitment: A Study of the Generation Gap* (Garden City, NY: Doubleday, 1970), p. 64.

Chapter 7: Judicial Schizophrenia

1. These early cases rested upon a Christian understanding of the marriage contract. The United States Supreme Court's opinion in *Maynard v. Hill*, 125 U.S. 190 (1888), is illustrative of this long line of precedent:

   > ... (W)hilst marriage is often termed by text writers and in decisions of courts a civil contract . . . it is something more than a mere contract. The consent of the parties is of course essential to its existence, but when the contract to marry is executed by the marriage, a relation between the parties is created which they cannot change. Other contracts may be modified, restricted, or enlarged, or entirely released upon the consent of the parties. Not so with marriage. The relation once formed, the law steps in and holds the parties to various obligations and liabilities. It is an institution, the maintenance of which in its purity the public is deeply interested, for it is the foundation of the family and of society, without which there would be neither civilization nor progress.

   Ibid., pp. 210, 211.
   Given this view of marriage as a "status" or "institution" and not merely as a "contract," the various tasks assigned to the family were protected from state encroachment. Thus, the Supreme Court from *Meyer v. Nebraska*, 262 U.S. 390 (1923), to *Moore v. City of East Cleveland*, 431 U.S. 494 (1977), could lay down rules of law that favored parental control over the education of their children and that favored familial choices in living arrangements. Even the question of the proper use of contraceptives was considered to belong to the family on the assumption that the appropriate authority over the intimate sexual life of the husband and wife was lodged in the family unit, not the state. See, for example, *Griswold v. Connecticut*, 381 U.S. 479 (1965).

2. 405 U.S. 438 (1972).

3. Peter J. Riga, "The Supreme Court's View of Marriage and the Family: Tradition or Transition?," *Journal of Family Law* 18, (1979-80) 301, 302-03, (footnote omitted). Riga further writes: "*Eisenstadt* . . . represents a radical departure with little or no constitutional foundation or development either in American legal history or in case law. . . . The tracings of constitutional theory affecting marriage have gone, in a little more than eight years, from the obscure but historical in *Griswold* to the unintelligible, unhistorical, and illogical in *Eisenstadt*." *Ibid.*, p. 303.

4. *Ibid.*, p. 304.

5. In *Roe v. Wade*, 410 U.S. 113 (1973), Justice Harry Blackmun relied upon *Meyer* in fashioning a right to privacy "broad enough to encompass a woman's decision whether or not to terminate her pregnancy":

   > The Constitution does not explicitly mention any right to privacy. In a line of decisions, however, . . . the Court has recognized that a right of . . . privacy . . . does exist under the Constitution. In varying contexts the Court . . . indeed found at least the roots of that right . . . in the concept of liberty guaranteed in the first section of the Fourteeneth Amendment, see *Meyer v. Nebraska*, 262 U.S. 390, 399 (1923).

   Ibid., p. 153.

6. The Court in *Roe* concluded that the permissibility of state regulation was to be viewed in three stages: "For the stage prior to approximately the end of the first trimester, the abortion decision and its effectuation must be left to the medical judgment of the pregnant woman's attending physician," without interference from the state. 410 U.S. at 164. After the first stage, as so described, the state may, if it chooses, reasonably regulate the abortion procedure to preserve and protect maternal health. *Ibid.* Finally, for the stage subsequent to viability the state may regulate an abortion to protect the life of the unborn child and even may proscribe abortion except where it is necessary for the preservation of the life or "health" of the mother. *Ibid.,* pp. 163-165.

7. The Court in *Roe* held:

> Maternity, or additional offspring, may force upon the woman a distressful life and future. Psychological harm may be imminent. Mental and physical health may be taxed by child care. There is also the distress, for all concerned, associated with the unwanted child, and there is the problem of bringing a child into a family already unable, psychologically and otherwise, to care for it. In other cases, as in this one, the additional difficulties and continuing stigma of unwed motherhood may be involved. All these are factors the woman and her responsible physician necessarily will consider in consultation.

410 U.S. at 153.

8. To those who would challenge this conclusion I would refer them to the annual average of 1.6 million plus abortions performed in the United States since the decision in *Roe* in 1973 as well as Justice White's dissent in *Planned Parenthood v. Danforth,* 428 U.S. 52, 92 (1976): "In *Roe v. Wade* . . . this Court recognized a right to an abortion free from state prohibition."

9. 428 U.S. 52 (1976).

10. *Ibid.,* pp. 69, 71. In holding that the law involved did not foster marital relationships, Blackmun noted that "we recognize that the decision to undergo or to forgo an abortion may have profound effects on the future of any marriage, effects that are both physical and mental, and possibly deleterious. Notwithstanding these factors, we cannot hold that the state has the constitutional authority to give the spouse unilaterally the ability to prohibit the wife from terminating her pregnancy, when the state itself lacks that right." *Ibid.,* p. 70.

11. *Ibid.,* p. 73.

12. *Ibid.,* p. 75. In the companion case to *Danforth, Bellotti v. Baird,* 428 U.S. 132 (1976), the Court found unconstitutional a state law requiring parental written consent before an abortion could be performed on an unmarried minor, even though the law provided that an abortion could be obtained under court order upon a showing of good cause if one or both parents refused consent. In *Bellotti II v. Baird,* 442 U.S. 622 (1979), the Court reaffirmed the unconstitutionality of the statute involved in *Bellotti I* but with some language favorable to the parents' role in the upbringing of children. *Ibid.,* pp. 633-639.

13. *Carey v. Population Services International,* 431 U.S. 678 (1977).

14. *Doe v. Irwin*, 428 F. Supp. 1198 (W.D. Mich. 1977), vacated without opinion, 559 F. 2d 1219 (6th Cir. 1977).
15. 450 U.S. 398 (1981).
16. 393 U.S. 503 (1969).
17. *Ibid.*, p. 511.
18. *Ibid.*, pp. 518, 522.
19. *Goss v. Lopez*, 419 U.S. 565 (1975).
20. The Court noted that suspension from a public school "is a serious event in the life of the suspended child. Neither the property interest in educational benefits temporarily denied nor the liberty interest in reputation, which is also implicated, is so insubstantial that suspensions may constitutionally be imposed by any procedure the school chooses, no matter how arbitrary." *Ibid.*, pp. 590, 591.
21. *Ibid.* (emphasis in original).
22. 428 U.S. at 74.
23. Bruce Hafen, "Puberty, Privacy, and Protection: The Risks of Children's 'Rights,' " *American Bar Association Journal* 63 (October 1977), 1383, 1385. Elsewhere it has been noted:

    > Also important is the view of the nature of marriage expressed in *Danforth*. Traditional marriage was a convenanted community formed from the consent of both parties and therefore something more profound than the individuals who composed it. On the other hand, *Danforth's* view of marriage follows that of *Eisenstadt*, that is, marriage is seen as a tenuous union formed by the consensual agreement of the two individuals who remain autonomous and independent throughout the relationship. Since this is so, then the decision to abort comes down on the autonomous individual who has the most to lose, gain, suffer, etc., in a sort of balancing process of advantages versus disadvantages. In this instance the woman does the balancing. No heed is given to the unbreakable unity or covenant, where the marital institution is greater than its composite individuals, because this no longer exists as a definition of marriage. The implicit view of marriage in *Eisenstadt* is directly responsible for the individual decision in *Danforth*. *Eisenstadt genuit Roe; Ambos genuerunt Danforth.*

    Op. cit., Riga, pp. 304, 305.
24. *Op. cit.*, Hafen, p. 1386.
25. *Ibid.*, p. 1388.
26. Comment, "Adjudicating What Yoder Left Unresolved: Religious Rights for Minor Children After Danforth and Carey," *Pennsylvania Law Review* 126 (1978), 1135, 1155.
27. *Ibid.* (footnotes omitted) (emphasis supplied). The writer goes on to state, "Children will have to continue to rely on state protection of their religious interests as against their parents, and of course any state efforts to vindicate their interests are limited by parental constitutional rights recognized in *Pierce* and *Yoder*. A case could arise if the state did seek to protect the religious rights of minors. This conflict would be between the child's state-supported interest in religious freedom (not the child's constitutional right) and the parents' constitutionally protected rights." *Ibid.*, p. 1159 (footnote omitted).
28. 532 P. 2d 278 (1975).

29. For example, see *In re Hanes*, 574 P. 2d 395 (1978); *In re Tarango*, 595 P. 2d 552 (1979); *In re Bennett*, 600 P. 2d 1308 (1979); *In re Clark*, 611 P. 2d 1343 (1980).
30. 532 P. 2d at 281.
31. *Ibid.*, p. 279.
32. Bruce Hafen, "Children's Liberties and the New Egalitarianism: Some Reservations About Abandoning Youth to Their Rights," *Brigham Young Law Review* (1976) 605, 609.
33. *Pierce v. Society of Sisters*, 268 U.S. 510, 535 (1923).
34. *Op. cit.*, Comment, pp. 1155-1158. Some courts have already recognized that adolescent children are sufficiently mature to meaningfully exercise the right to choose among competing religious beliefs. This is reflected in a number of custody dispute cases where children have been allowed to make their own choice on the issue of religion. For example, in *Hehman v. Hehman*, 13 Misc. 2d 318, 178 N.Y.S. 2d 328 (Sup. Ct. 1958), a New York court ordered that a dispute between parents as to a child's religious upbringing be referred to an official referee, who would interview the thirteen-year-old boy involved to determine his own religious preference. The court noted the boy's age and the fact that he had been exposed to both his parents' creeds. *Ibid.* at 321, 178 N.Y.S. 2d at 331. The *Hehman* court concluded that the decision should be left to the child who could not "be forced to enter a religion against his wishes." *Ibid. Op. cit.*, Comment, pp. 1157, 1158.
35. Laurence Tribe, "Childhood, Suspect Classifications, and Conclusive Presumptions: Three Linked Riddles," *Law and Contemporary Problems* 39 (1975) 8, 35.
36. See John W. Whitehead, *The Second American Revolution* (Elgin, IL: David C. Cook, 1982).
37. George Orwell, *Nineteen Eighty-Four* (New York: Harcourt, Brace and World, 1949), pp. 136, 137.

Chapter 8: The Conflict in Education

1. Samuel Blumenfeld, *Is Public Education Necessary?* (Old Greenwich, CT: Devin-Adair, 1981), p. 9.
2. *Ibid.*, p. x.
3. John W. Whitehead, *The Second American Revolution* (Elgin, IL: David C. Cook, 1982), pp. 96, 97.
4. *A Declaration of the Rights of the Inhabitants of the Commonwealth of Massachusetts* (1919), Art. 3, Sec. 2.
5. For example, James Madison termed religion as "the duty which we owe to our Creator, and the manner of discharging it." In particular, Madison's fear was that the legislation to which he was opposed (a tax levied to pay the salaries of teachers of the Christian religion) in his *Remonstrance* would be adverse to the diffusion of the light of Christianity. James Madison, *Memorial*

and Remonstrance on the Religious Rights of Man (1784), as reprinted in Donald Manzullo, *Neither Sacred Nor Profane* (Jericho, NY: Exposition Press, 1973), p. 76. Also see Whitehead and Conlan, "The Establishment of the Religion of Secular Humanism and Its First Amendment Implications," *Texas Tech Law Review* 10 (1978), 1.

6. Terry Eastland, "In Defense of Religious America," *Commentary* (June 1981), p. 40.

7. Jonathan Messerli, *Horace Mann: A Biography* (New York: Knopf, 1972), p. xii.

8. A detailed discussion of the philosophy of the leading characters in the development of American public education is provided in Rousas J. Rush-doony, *The Messianic Character of American Education* (Nutley, NJ: Craig Press, 1963).

9. *Op. cit.*, Messerli, p. xii.

10. John Dewey, *A Common Faith* (New Haven, CT: Yale University Press, 1934), p. 84.

11. John Dewey, *My Pedagogic Creed* (Washington, D.C.: Progressive Education Association, 1897), pp. 6, 15, 17.

12. Allan Bloom, "Our Listless Universities," *National Review* (December 10, 1982), p. 1537.

13. *Ibid.*

14. William Shirer, *The Rise and Fall of the Third Reich* (New York: Simon & Schuster, 1960), p. 249.

15. William V. Shannon, "Too Much, Too Soon," *New York Times* (September 8, 1976), p. 37.

16. "Help! Teacher Can't Teach!" *Time* (June 16, 1980), p. 54.

17. "Why Public Schools Fail," *Newsweek* (April 20, 1981), p. 62.

18. H. W. Koch, *Hitler Youth: The Duped Generation* (New York: Ballantine Books, 1972), p. 10.

19. *Op. cit.*, Bloom, p. 1537.

20. Roger Waters, *Another Brick in the Wall* (Pink Floyd Music Ltd., 1979).

21. *Op. cit.*, Shirer, p. 249.

22. *Ibid.*, p. 255.

23. *Op. cit.*, Koch, p. 104.

24. Since the Christian school movement is of recent origin, there are few statis-tics comparing student performance in the public schools as opposed to that in private Christian schools. What is important at this point are the statistics which do exist, and in most instances they uniformly indicate that Christian schools are producing superior students academically.

    Dr. Paul A. Kienel, executive director of the Association of Christian Schools International, has reported on surveys his organization has conduct-ed. His findings show that Christian schools are making significant academic gains as opposed to public schools. "Stanford Achievement test scores have improved from 6 to 16 months ahead of the national norm (in grades 1-8) in 1973 and 7 to 19 months ahead of the national norm in 1975. The same association-wide testing program showed an increase in all subject areas from 5 to 9 months ahead of the national norm to 6 to 13 months ahead in grades one through eight over the same two-year period. Similar academic gains were experienced at the high school level." Jon Barton and John Whitehead, *Schools on Fire* (Wheaton, IL: Tyndale House, 1980), p. 49. Recent research lends support to these statistics. See James S. Coleman, Thomas Hoffer, and Sally Kilgore, *High School Achievement* (New York: Basic Books, 1982).

25. James Carper, "Rendering Unto Caesar: A Perspective on Christian Day Schools, State Regulation, and the First Amendment," paper presented to the American Educational Studies Association (November 4, 1982), p. 18.

26. This case has been heavily criticized in Commentary, "Douglas v. Faith Baptist Church: Under Constitutional Scrutiny," *Nebraska Law Review* 61 (1982), 74.

27. John Naisbitt, *Megatrends: Ten New Directions Transforming Our Lives* (New York: Warner Books, 1982), p. 144. Also see Raymond and Dorothy Moore, *Home Grown Kids: A Practical Handbook for Teaching Your Children at Home* (Waco, TX: Word Books, 1981).

28. Alvin Toffler, *The Third Wave* (New York: Morrow, 1980), p. 386.

29. Paul Blanshard, "Three Cheers for Our Secular State," *The Humanist* (March/April 1976), p. 17.

30. G. Richard Bozarth, "On Keeping God Alive," *The American Atheist* (November 1977), p. 7.

31. John J. Dunphy, "A Religion for a New Age," *The Humanist* (January/February 1983), p. 26 (emphasis supplied).

Chapter 9: Subduing the Church

1. R. J. Rushdoony, "Taxation," *Chalcedon Position Paper*, No. 21, p. 3.

2. Erik von Kuehnelt-Leddihn, *Leftism: From de Sade and Marx to Hitler and Marcuse* (New Rochelle, NY: Arlington House, 1974), p. 427.

3. Jan Pit, *Persecution: It Will Never Happen Here?* (Orange, CA: Open Doors, 1981), pp. 42, 43.

4. John A. Armstrong, *Ideology, Politics, and Government in the Soviet Union* (New York: Praeger, 1974), p. 129.

Chapter 10: Priorities and Resistance

1. As quoted in Jan Pit, *Persecution: It Will Never Happen Here?* (Orange, CA: Open Doors, 1981), p. 17 (emphasis in original).

2. Harry Blamires, *The Christian Mind* (Ann Arbor, MI: Servant Books, 1978), p. 3.

3. Ed Briggs, "Only 1 in 10 Held Deeply Committed," *Richmond Times-Dispatch* (November 27, 1982), p. B-3.

4. Kenneth L. Woodward and David Gates, "How the Bible Made America," *Newsweek* (December 27, 1982), p. 45.

5. William Barclay, *The Ten Commandments for Today* (Grand Rapids, MI: Eerdmans, 1973), p. 9.
6. *Ibid.*
7. C. S. Lewis, *God in the Dock* (Grand Rapids, MI: Eerdmans, 1971), p. 262.
8. Brother Andrew, *The Ethics of Smuggling* (Wheaton, IL: Tyndale House, 1974), p. 18.
9. Os Guinness, *The Dust of Death* (Downers Grove, IL: InterVarsity Press, 1973), pp. 177, 178.
10. Jim Buchfuehrer, "Action Alternatives," *Plan for Action: An Action Alternative Handbook for Whatever Happened to the Human Race?* (Old Tappan, NJ: Revell, 1980), p. 17.
11. *Op. cit.*, Barclay, p. 59.
12. See Robin Lloyd, *For Money or Love: Boy Prostitution in America* (New York: Vanguard Press, 1976).
13. Leonard Peikoff, *The Ominous Parallels: The End of Freedom in America* (New York: Stein and Day, 1982), p. 7.
14. As quoted by B. F. Skinner, *Beyond Freedom and Dignity* (New York: Knopf, 1971), p. 34.
15. Rousas John Rushdoony, *Law and Liberty* (Nutley, NJ: Craig Press, 1971), p. 74.
16. Malcolm Muggeridge, *Christ and the Media* (Grand Rapids, MI: Eerdmans, 1977), p. 82. Also see Franky Schaeffer, *Addicted to Mediocrity* (Westchester, IL: Crossway Books, 1981).
17. Ron Jenson, *Together We Can Deal with Life in the 80s* (San Bernardino, CA: Here's Life, 1982), p. 78.
18. See generally Helen Gurley Brown, *Having It All* (New York: Simon and Schuster, 1982).
19. George Gilder, *Sexual Suicide* (New York: Quadrangle, 1973), p. 18.
20. Deborah Fallows, "My Turn: What Day Care Can't Do," *Newsweek* (January 10, 1983), p. 8.
21. Richard Wurmbrand, *Tortured for Christ* (Glendale, CA: Diane Books, 1967), p. 15.
22. *Ibid.*, p. 16.
23. *Ibid.*
24. *Ibid.*, p. 83.
25. *Op. cit.*, Brother Andrew, p. 95.
26. *Op. cit.*, Wurmbrand, p. 37.
27. *Ibid.*, pp. 36, 37.
28. Jean-Paul Sartre, *Existentialism and Human Emotions* (New York: Philosophical Library, 1947), p. 23.
29. *Op cit.*, Barclay, p. 13.

REFERENCES

Abbott, Sidney and Love, Barbara. *Sappho Was a Right-On Woman: A Liberated View of Lesbianism.* New York: Stein and Day, 1972.

"Abortion Found Safer than Giving Birth." *Washington Post,* July 9, 1982.

Alexander, Brooks. "The Rise of Cosmic Humanism: What is Religion?" *SCP Journal,* Winter 1981-82.

American Political Report, August 17, 1979, p. 3.

Andrew Brother. *The Ethics of Smuggling.* Wheaton, IL: Tyndale House, 1974.

Armstrong, John A. *Ideology, Politics and Government in the Soviet Union.* New York: Praeger, 1974.

Barclay, William. *The Ten Commandments for Today.* Grand Rapids, MI: Eerdmans, 1973.

Baynes, N. H., ed. *The Speeches of Adolf Hitler, 1922-39.* 2 vols. London: Oxford University Press, 1942.

Begley, Sharon. "Nature's Baby Killers." *Newsweek,* September 6, 1982.

Bird, Wendell. "Freedom of Religion and Science Instruction in Public Schools." *Yale Law Journal* 87 (1976), 515.

Blamires, Harry. *The Christian Mind.* Ann Arbor, MI: Servant Books, 1978.

Blanshard, Paul. "Three Cheers for Our Secular State." *The Humanist,* March/April 1976.

Bloom, Allan, "Our Listless Universities." *National Review,* December 10, 1982.

Blumenfeld, Samuel. *Is Public Education Necessary?* Old Greenwich, CT: Devin-Adair, 1981.

Bork, Robert. "The Struggle Over the Role of the Court." *National Review*, September 17, 1982.

Bozarth, Richard G. "On Keeping God Alive." *The American Atheist*, November 1977.

Bredemeier, Harry C. and Stephenson, Richard M. *The Analysis of Social Systems*. New York: Holt, Rinehart, and Winston, 1962.

Briggs, Ed. "Only 1 in 10 Held Deeply Committed." *Richmond-Times Dispatch*, November 27, 1982.

Brinston, Crane and Christopher, John B. and Wolff, Robert Lee. *A History of Civilization*. 2 vols. 2nd ed. Englewood Cliffs, NJ: Prentice-Hall, 1963.

Bronfenbrenner, Urie. "The Disturbing Changes in the American Family." *Search*, Fall 1976 (as reprinted in *The Journal of Christian Reconstruction*, IV, Winter 1977-78).

Brown, Helen Gurley. *Having It All*. New York: Simon and Schuster, 1982.

Buchfuehrer, Jim. "Action Alternatives." *Plan for Action: An Action Alternative Handbook for Whatever Happened to the Human Race?* Old Tappan, NJ: Revell, 1980.

Burtchaell, James Tunstead. *Rachael Weeping and Other Essays on Abortion*. Fairway, KS: Andrews and McMeel, 1982.

———. "The Holocaust and Abortion." Supplement to *Catholic League Newsletter*, Vol. 9, No. 11.

Carper, James. "Rendering Unto Caesar: A Perspective on Christian Day Schools, State Regulation, and the First Amendment." A paper presented to the American Educational Studies Association, November 4, 1982.

Chase, Allan. *The Legacy of Malthus: The Social Costs of the New Scientific Racism*. New York: Knopf, 1976.

Clark, Robert E. *Darwin: Before and After*. London: Paternoster, 1948.

Coleman, James S. *The Adolescent Society*. New York: Free Press, 1971.

———, Hoffer, Thomas and Kilgore, Sally. *High School Achievement*. New York: Basic Books, 1982.

Coleman, Laura and Waters, David. "Controversy Over Nazis Raises Fears." *The Commercial Appeal*, November 17, 1982.

Colorado Springs Gazette Telegraph, December 16, 1981, p. 9-C.

Comment. "Adjudicating What Yoder Left Unresolved: Religious Rights for Minor Children After Danforth and Carey." *Pennsylvania Law Review* 126 (1978), 1135.

Commentary. "Douglas v. Faith Baptist Church: Under Constitutional Scrutiny," *Nebraska Law Review* 61 (1982), 74.

Conway, J. S. *The Nazi Persecution of the Church, 1933-45.* New York: Basic Books, 1968.

"Court Affirms $178,000 for Va. Couple." *Washington Post,* May 1, 1982.

Cox, Harvey. *The Secular City.* New York: Macmillan, 1965.

Danielski, Daniel J. and Tulchin, Joseph S., ed. *The Autobiographical Notes of Charles Evans Hughes.* Cambridge, MA: Harvard University Press, 1973.

Darwin, Charles. *The Origin of the Species by Means of Natural Selection or the Preservation of Favoured Races in the Struggle for Life* (1859). New York: Oxford University Press, 1963.

"Death of the Family." *Newsweek,* January 17, 1983.

Dewey, John. *A Common Faith.* New Haven, CT: Yale University Press, 1934.

————. *Characters and Events: Popular Essays in Social and Political Philosophy.* New York: Holt, 1929.

————. *My Pedagogic Creed.* Washington, D.C.: Progressive Education Association, 1897.

Diamond, David A. "The First Amendment and Public Schools: The Case Against Judicial Intervention." *Texas Law Review* 59 (1981), 477.

"Doctor Sees Trend Not to Resuscitate." *Washington Post,* June 12, 1982.

"Doctor's Dilemma: Treat or Let Die." *U.S. News and World Report,* December 6, 1982.

Dunphy, John J. "A Religion for a New Age." *The Humanist,* January/February 1983.

Eastland, Terry. "In Defense of Religious America." *Commentary,* June 1981.

"Economy Cited by Many as Reason for Abortion." *Presbyterian Journal,* November 17, 1982.

Edwards, Newton. *The Courts and the Public Schools.* 3rd ed. Chicago: University of Chicago Press, 1971.

Elkind, David. *The Hurried Child.* Reading, MA: Addison-Wesley, 1981.

Ellul, Jacques. *The Political Illusion.* New York: Vintage Press, 1972.

"Europe's Anti-Semitism." *Newsweek,* August 23, 1982.

Fallows, Deborah. "My Turn: What Day Care Can't Do." *Newsweek,* January 10, 1983.

Fleetwood, Blake. "The Tax Police: Trampling Citizens' Rights." *Saturday Review,* May 1980.

Gilder, George. *Sexual Suicide.* New York: Quadrangle Books, 1973.

Gladstone, Mark. "Evidence Sought in Death of Fetuses." *Los Angeles Times,* February 7, 1982.

Gould, Stephen J. *The Mismeasure of Man.* New York: W. W. Norton, 1981.

Greenberg, Joel. "B. F. Skinner Now Sees Little Hope for the World's Salvation." *New York Times,* September 15, 1981.

Gross, Bertram. *Friendly Fascism: The New Face of Power in America.* New York: M. Evans, 1980.

Guinness, Os. *The Dust of Death.* Downers Grove, IL: InterVarsity Press, 1973.

Hafen, Bruce. "Children's Liberties and the New Egalitarianism: Some Reservations About Abandoning Youth to Their Rights." *Brigham Young Law Review* (1976), 605.

_____. "Puberty, Privacy, and Protection: The Risks of Child's 'Rights.'" *American Bar Association Journal* 63 (October 1977), 1383.

Hegel, Georg Wilhelm Friedrich. *Philosophy of Right.* Trans. T. M. Knox. London: Oxford Press. 1967.

_____. *The Philosophy of History.* Trans. J. Sibree. Rev. ed. New York: Colonial Press, 1900.

"Help! Teacher Can't Teach." *Time,* June 16, 1980.

Hertz, Richard. *Chance and Symbol.* Chicago: University of Chicago Press, 1948.

Hitchcock, James. *What Is Secular Humanism?* Ann Arbor, MI: Servant Books, 1982.

Hitler, Adolf. *Mein Kampf.* (1925). New York: Houghton Mifflin, 1971.

Hubel, David H. "The Brain." *Scientific American,* September 1979.

Hunt, Richard M. "No-Fault Guilt-Free History." *New York Times,* February 16, 1976.

Huntford, Roland. *The New Totalitarians.* New York: Stein and Day, 1972.

Huxley, Aldous. *Brave New World.* (1939). New York: Bantam Books, 1968.

Huxley, Julian, "Evolution and Genetics," in *What is Science?* J. R. Newman, ed. New York: Simon and Schuster, 1955.

Ingber, Dina. "Brain Breathing." *Science Digest,* June 1981.

Jenson, Ron. *Together We Can Deal With Life in the 80s.* San Bernardino, CA: Here's Life, 1982.

Johnson, Lloyd and Bachman, Jerald and O'Malley, Patrick. "Student Drug Use in America, 1975-1980." National Institute on Drug Abuse, Rockville, Maryland.

Keith, Arthur. *Evolution and Ethics.* New York: G. P. Putnam's Sons, 1949.

Koch, H. W. *Hitler Youth: The Duped Generation.* New York: Ballantine, 1972.

Kolnai, Aurel. *The War Against the West.* New York: Viking Press, 1938.

Kuehnelt-Leddihn, Erik von. *Leftism: From de Sade and Marx to Hitler and Marcuse.* New Rochelle, NY: Arlington House, 1974.

Lewis, C. S. *God in the Dock.* Grand Rapids, MI: Eerdmans, 1971.

Lloyd, Robin. *For Money or Love: Boy Prostitution in America.* New York: Vanguard Press, 1976.

Loftus, John. *The Belarus Secret.* New York: Knopf, 1982.

Long, Mary. "Visions of a New Faith." *Science Digest,* November 1981.

"Looking Ahead: Nine Top Women Eye the Future." *Working Women,* December 1982.

Mankiewicz, Frank and Swedlow, Joel. *Remote Control.* New York: Ballantine, 1979.

Marriott, Michael and Rimer, Sara. "Adult-Oriented Washington Area Leads U.S. Life-Style Changes." *Washington Post*, November 7, 1982.

Margen, Thomas J. "Aborted Babies Born at Hospital With 'Model' Eugenics Program." *National Right to Life News*, May 20, 1982.

Matheson, Peter. *The Third Reich and the Christian Churches*. Grand Rapids, MI: Eerdmans, 1981.

McLuhan, Marshall. "Cybernation and Culture." *The Social Impact of Cybernetics*. New York: Simon and Schuster, 1966.

Mead, Margaret. *Culture and Commitment: A Study of the Generation Gap*. Garden City, NY: Doubleday, 1970.

Messerli, Jonathan. *Horace Mann: A Biography*. New York: Knopf, 1972.

Moore, Raymond and Dorothy. *Home Grown Kids: A Practical Handbook for Teaching Your Children at Home*. Waco, TX: Word, 1981.

Muggeridge, Malcolm. *Christ and the Media*. Grand Rapids, MI: Eerdmans, 1977.

_____. *The End of Christendom*. Grand Rapids, MI: Eerdmans, 1980.

Naisbitt, John. *Megatrends: Ten New Directions Transforming Our Lives*. New York: Warner Books, 1982.

Nathanson, Bernard, M.D. *Aborting America*. Garden City, NY: Doubleday, 1979.

New York Times Book Review, February 25, 1973, p. 39.

North, Gary. *None Dare Call It Witchcraft*. New Rochelle, NY: Arlington House, 1976.

Novak, Michael. *The Spirit of Democratic Capitalism*. New York: American Enterprise Institute/Simon and Schuster, 1982.

O'Brien, Glen. "Notes on the Neon Nihilists." *High Times*, November 1980.

"One in Six U.S. Babies Born Out of Wedlock." *Washington Post*, October 27, 1981.

Orwell, George. *Nineteen Eighty-Four*. New York: Harcourt, Brace and World, 1949.

Peikoff, Leonard. "A Sense of Inevitability." *King Features Syndicate*, May 22, 1979.

————. *The Ominous Parallels: The End of Freedom in America.* Briarcliff, NY: Stein and Day, 1982.

Phillips, Kevin P. *Post-Conservative America: People, Politics, and Ideology in a Time of Crisis.* New York, Random House, 1981.

"Philosopher Proposes Euthanasia for Severely Disabled Infants." *Newport News Daily Press,* January 10, 1982.

Pit, Jan. *Persecution: It Will Never Happen Here?* Orange, CA: Open Doors, 1981.

"Population of Singles Rising, Census Reports." *Washington Post,* October 19, 1981.

"Post-Abortion Fetal Study Stirs Storm." *Medical World News,* June 8, 1972.

Postman, Neil. *The Disappearance of Childhood.* New York: Delacorte Press, 1982.

Press, Aric. "Divorce American Style." *Newsweek,* January 10, 1983

Rich, Spencer. "Single-Parent Families Rise Dramatically." *Washington Post,* May 3, 1982.

Riga, Peter J. "The Supreme Court's View of Marriage and the Family: Tradition or Transition?" *Journal of Family Law* 18 (1979-80), 301.

Rookmaaker, H. R. *Modern Art and the Death of a Culture.* Downers Grove, IL: InterVarsity Press, 1970.

Rushdoony, Rousas J. *Law and Liberty.* Nutley, NJ: Craig Press, 1971.

————. "Taxation." *Chalcedon Position Paper,* No. 21.

————. *The Messianic Character of American Education.* Nutley, NJ: Craig Press, 1963.

Russell, Cristine. "Scientist's Review of '70s Abortions 'Largely Positive.' " *Washington Post,* March 19, 1982.

Sartre, Jean-Paul. *Existentialism and Human Emotions.* New York: Philosophical Library, 1947.

Satchell, Michael. "Fear the IRS." *Parade,* April 12, 1981.

Schaeffer, Francis A. *A Christian Manifesto.* Westchester, IL: Crossway Books, 1981.

————. *How Should We Then Live?* Old Tappan, NJ: Revell, 1976.

_____ and Koop, C. Everett. *Whatever Happened to the Human Race?* Old Tappan, NJ: Revell, 1979.

Schaeffer, Franky. *A Time for Anger: The Myth of Neutrality.* Westchester, IL: Crossway Books, 1982.

_____. *Addicted to Mediocrity.* Westchester, IL: Crossway Books, 1981.

Schwartz, Michael. "Abortion: The Nazi Connection." *Catholic League Newsletter,* August 1978.

"Sexual Portrayals Using Children Legal Unless Obscene, Court Rules." *New York Times,* May 13, 1981.

Shannon, William V. "Too Much, Too Soon." *New York Times,* September 8, 1976.

Shirer, William. *The Rise and Fall of the Third Reich.* New York: Simon and Schuster, 1960.

Skinner, B. F. *Beyond Freedom and Dignity.* New York: Knopf, 1971.

Skylar, Dusty. *God and Beasts: Nazis and the Occult.* New York: Crowell, 1977.

Spengler, Oswald. *The Decline of the West, 1918-22.* 2 vols. New York: Knopf, 1945.

The Connecticut Mutual Life Report on American Values in the '80s: The Impact of Belief. Hartford, CT: Connecticut Mutual Life Insurance Company, 1981.

Thimmesch, Nick. "Fetuses and Cosmetics: The French Connection." *Los Angeles Times Syndicate,* 1982.

Thompson, William Irwin. " 'What's Past is Prologue,' The Past—What's That?" *New York Times,* June 10, 1976.

Toffler, Alvin. *The Third Wave.* New York: Morrow, 1980.

Tribe, Laurence. "Childhood, Suspect Classifications, and Conclusive Presumptions: Three Linked Riddles." *Law and Contemporary Problems* 39 (1975), 8.

Ventura, Stephanie. "Teenage Childbearing: United States, 1966-1975." *The Monthly Vital Statistics Report,* National Center for Health Statistics.

Verny, Thomas. *The Secret Life of the Unborn Child.* New York: Summit Books, 1981.

Vibbert, Spencer. "Punk, Boston Style." *Boston Globe Magazine,* March 2, 1980.

Virekananda, Swami. *Inspired Talks.* New York: Ramakrishna Virekananda Center, 1958.

Waters, Roger. *Another Brick in the Wall.* Pink Floyd Music, Ltd., 1979.

Weitzman, Lenore. "Changing Families, Changing Laws." *Family Advocate,* Summer 1982.

"Why Public Schools Fail." *Newsweek,* April 20, 1981.

Wilder-Smith, A. E. *He Who Thinks Has to Believe.* Minneapolis: Bethany House, 1981.

Will, George F. "Abortion Does Cause Pain to Its Victims." *Washington Post,* November 5, 1981.

Woodward, Kenneth L. and Gates, David. "How the Bible Made America." *Newsweek,* December 27, 1982.

Wurmbrand, Richard. *Tortured for Christ.* Glendale, CA: Diane Books, 1967.

INDEX